VIOLENCE WITHOUT BORDERS: THE INTERNATIONALIZATION OF CRIME AND CONFLICT

ISBN (paper): 978-1-4648-1452-5
ISBN (electronic): 978-1-4648-1525-6
DOI: 10.1596/978-1-4648-1452-5

Cover photo: The former frontline area of Kobani, where Kurdish fighters battled ISIS in 2014, lies in ruins nearly five years after the conflict. The Turkish border wall, which now marks the new front line between Kurdish Syrian forces and Turkey, is less than 200 meters away at points. © Ivor Prickett/NY Times/Panos Pictures. Used with the permission of Ivor Prickett/NY Times/Panos Pictures. Further permission required for reuse.
Cover design: Bill Pragluski, Critical Stages, Inc.

Library of Congress Control Number: 2020932954

Contents

Foreword   ix

Acknowledgments   xi

Executive Summary   xiii

Abbreviations   xvii

Overview   1
  Notes   5
  Reference   5

1. Crime, Conflict, and Violence without Borders   7
  Armed conflict   8
  Transnational terrorism   18
  Illicit markets   21
  Conclusion   30
  Annex 1A The geographic dispersion of refugees   31
  Notes   35
  References   37

2. Transborder Determinants of Crime, Conflict, and Violence   43
  The theoretical framework   44
  Transborder drivers of conflict, crime, and violence   50
  Can violence be avoided?   57
  Foreign military interventions and development assistance   61
  Conclusion   71
  Annex 2A Contest model   71
  Notes   75
  References   77

3. Security in a Globalized World   89
    Third-party interventions to prevent violence   89
    When will other countries intervene in conflict situations?   91
    Limits to the effectiveness of third-party interventions   102
    Multilateralism and the delegation of foreign interventions   104
    Concluding remarks and policy recommendations   106
    Annex 3A The determinants of foreign interventions
        in civil conflict   110
    Notes   118
    References   119

Boxes
1.1   The gaps and data limitations of datasets on armed conflicts   9
2.1   Sanctions   62
2.2   Anti-money laundering and combatting the financing of terrorism   63

Figures
1.1   Armed conflicts: Incidence and fatalities, by type, 1989–2017   11
1.2   State-based armed conflicts, by type, 1946–2017   11
1.3   All armed conflicts, by type, 1989–2017   12
1.4   Global refugee population, 1951–2017   14
1.5   Average distance traveled by a refugee, 1987–2017   15
1.6   Share of refugees going to a contiguous country, 1987–2017   16
1.7   Mean Herfindahl index of destinations, five-year moving average,
        1991–2017   17
1.8   Terrorist attacks and fatalities worldwide, 1970–2017   19
1.9   Transnational terrorist attacks and fatalities, 1970–2017   21
1.10 Cultivation and production of illicit narcotics, 1986–2017   23
1.11 Trends in detection of human trafficking, 2003–16   25
1.12 Domestic poaching incidents and transnational seizures   27
1.13 Piracy attacks, 1991–2018   28
1A.1 Average distance traveled by a refugee, five-year moving average,
        1991–2017   32
1A.2 Share of refugees going to a contiguous country, five-year moving
        average, 1991–2017   32
1A.3 Refugees fleeing to wealthy OECD and European countries, five-year
        moving average   35
2.1   Equilibrium in a contest game   46
2.2   Determinants of violence in the contest success function model   48
2.3   Contest game and the cone of possible resource allocations   58
3.1   Trends in United Nations peacekeeping operations and global aid flows,
        1947–2017   91
3.2   Intrastate wars and the number of foreign countries intervening,
        1990–2017   95
3.3   Likelihood of foreign interventions over time, 1990–2017   96

3.4   Drivers of foreign interventions in civil wars   99
3.5   Probability that a war will continue and probability of foreign
        intervention, by length of war   102

Tables

1.1   Global proceeds from transnational organized criminal networks   22
3A.1   Drivers of foreign interventions in civil wars   113
3A.2   Results by contiguity and post-9/11 occurrence .   117

Foreword

Globalization has helped raise the living standards of the citizens of developed and developing countries alike. Nowhere is this more evident than in the extraordinary progress made in poverty reduction over the past 20-30 years, which would not have been possible without global market integration. Globalization means that goods and services, labor and capital, and knowledge and information flow increasingly seamlessly across national borders.

Despite its aggregate benefits, global market integration is not an unmitigated force for good. It may exacerbate inequality and can result in increased pressure on natural resources and the environment. This Policy Research Report (PRR) highlights how crime, conflict, and violence can also spill across borders in an interconnected world. Outside actors often intervene in armed conflict within countries, a significant fraction of terrorist attacks are transnational, refugees travel longer distances to seek protection, and the global market for illicit goods continues to be sizeable.

The report unpacks the political economy of crime, conflict, and violence, the understanding of which is critical for the effectiveness of humanitarian, development, and security assistance. This knowledge is invaluable, particularly when there is a risk that ouside actors may destabilize an already volatile situation.

In addition, this PRR emphasizes the high cost imposed on countries around the globe by cross-border spillovers of crime and violence. Global spillovers require coordinated efforts at a global scale to address them, to ensure that the preconditions for development of peace and stability have a chance to take hold.

While this report was completed before the COVID-19 pandemic struck, its main messages carry added weight in the current context–viruses know no country borders either. The global public good nature of infectious disease prevention and mitigation has seldom been as conspicuous as it is today.

I believe that this report will be a useful resource for policy makers and scholars of conflict and international crime. Its thesis–that the global community has a large stake in preventing and resolving conflict, crime, and violence–will hopefully expand policy discussions beyond individual countries to regional and global solutions.

Aart Kraay
Director of Research
World Bank Group

Acknowledgments

This Policy Research Report was authored by a team comprising Muhammad Faisal Ali Baig, Quy-Toan Do, Daniel Garrote-Sanchez, Lakshmi Iyer, Chau Le, and Andrei Levchenko.

The report is sponsored by the World Bank's Development Research Group and has been carried out under the supervision of Shantayanan Devarajan and Simeon Djankov, Senior Directors of Development Economics; and Asli Demirgüç-Kunt and Aart Kraay, Directors of Research. Francisco H. G. Ferreira read, commented on, and corrected multiple versions of the draft; his contributions are too many to list.

Many other people provided invaluable feedback during the process. We would like to thank our peer reviewers Xavier Devictor, Philip Keefer, Caglar Özden, and Jacob Shapiro. Franck Bousquet was the discussant during internal consultation and provided critical feedback. We gratefully acknowledge comments from participants during the review of this report, in particular Amat Alsoswa, Jishnu Das, Damien de Walque, Stuti Khemani, Daniel Lederman, Shiva Makki, Aaditya Mattoo, Harun Onder, Berk Özler, and Martin Rama.

The World Bank's Formal Publishing Unit coordinated the report design, typesetting, printing, and dissemination. We are grateful to Aziz Gökdemir, Patricia Katayama, and especially Stephen Pazdan for handling a demanding production schedule with great efficiency. The report was professionally edited by Anne Grant and Nora Mara. Anna Regina Bonfield provided effective administrative support that allowed the process to flow smoothly. Ryan Douglas Hahn worked with us from the beginning until the end, helping us with every stage of framing and disseminating the ideas in this report. He worked tirelessly with Chisako Fukuda on communication and dissemination.

Executive Summary

With the increasing internationalization of conflict, crime, and violence, domestic political stability and law enforcement capability have now become regional and global public goods.

This report documents how permeable country borders have become in many different domains, and the troubling human and economic costs. The geographical spillovers of conflict and crime and political instability have intensified. Violence from armed conflict generates larger flows of refugees, who travel greater distances to seek protection and are distributed widely across many more receiving countries. In just 10 years, the number of transnational terrorist attacks has quintupled. The global trade in opium, cocaine, and other illicit drugs has reached a 30-year high, with production concentrated in a handful of countries. Elephant and rhinoceros killings are far above their 2000 levels because of persistent demand for wildlife products, and piracy in international waters is still a significant threat.

The increasing internationalization of crime and conflict is also reflected in their transnational determinants: (1) international demand and supply shocks for the major products a country produces; (2) foreign regulations (such as on illicit goods and services) that affect returns to producers and consumers along the supply chain; (3) technology diffusion; and (4) "conflict contagion" through either flows of tangible resources across borders (such as arms, fighters, and money) or flows of intangible resources (such as ideas, inspirations, and grievances).

Because political stability and law enforcement are, increasingly, global public goods, this provides a rationale for greater international assistance to countries facing fiscal and technical constraints that prevent them from providing stability and the rule of law. In a world where individual countries are sovereign, this report examines instruments of international assistance to alter the domestic social, political, and economic landscape. The report finds that the impact of foreign interventions (whether military interventions or development assistance) on violence is ambiguous and context-specific. Military interventions might increase the state's ability to control crime and insurgency but might also worsen citizens' attitudes toward the government. Similarly, foreign aid might improve livelihoods and thus provide youth with an alternative to violence. At the same time, foreign aid could have ambiguous effects on broader citizen support for the government: although aid can support a strategy of buying "hearts and minds," it can also aggravate corruption or generate retaliation and sabotage by criminal gangs or insurgent groups.

The challenge of collective prevention of internationalized conflict, crime, and violence is compounded by the "free-riding" problem: no single country internalizes the full regional and global benefits of supporting a fragile state in its maintenance of peace and the rule of law, which leads to the underprovision of assistance. Multilateral institutions can play an important role in institutionalizing such collective arrangements while recognizing the possibility of competing interests between nations permeating multilateral institutions.

Global institutions have a role to play in the provision of security. The report identifies areas of relevance for multilateral institutions:

1. *Generating data and knowledge for better policies.* The systematic collection of data on crime and conflict is a cornerstone of policy and research analysis for evidence-based policy making. The body of knowledge available to policy makers is heavily influenced by the data accessible for analysis. Given the public good nature of data, multilateral organizations have a comparative advantage in collecting data on crime and violence, and in making it available for academic and policy research. Innovation should be encouraged to alleviate the difficulty of data collection in violent or illegal settings.

2. *Delivering financial aid and technical expertise.* An individual country's political stability and ability to enforce laws have positive regional or global spillovers. In such cases, regional or global organizations can be suitable institutions to which countries delegate some aspects of their foreign policies so as to mitigate the collective action problem. Appropriate financial and knowledge instruments should then be designed to reflect the needs associated with and spillovers stemming from the provision of security and rule of law. This report also

highlights the challenges associated with upholding the "do-no-harm" principle in volatile contexts and underscores the complementarity between aid and security as an important aspect of development assistance in fragile settings.

3. *Providing a forum for policy coordination.* In an increasingly interconnected world, policies in one country can have a "beggar-thy-neighbor" effect on other countries with implications for the levels of conflict, crime, and violence, hence giving a transnational dimension to the "do-no-harm" principle. When policies are interdependent, multilateral institutions can provide a platform for coordination and collective bargaining to identify policies that are most desirable from a regional or global standpoint.

Abbreviations

ACLED	Armed Conflict Location & Event Data Project
AML/CFT	anti-money laundering and combatting the financing of terrorism
BAAD	Big, Allied, and Dangerous (dataset)
BRDs	battlefield-related deaths
CEN	Customs Enforcement Network
CERAC	Conflict Analysis Resource Center Database of the Armed Conflict (Colombia)
CITES	Convention on International Trade in Endangered Species of Wild Fauna and Flora
CoW	Correlates of War
DAC	Development Assistance Committee (OECD)
DDR	demobilization, disarmament, and reintegration
ETIS	Elephant Trade Information System
FATF	Financial Action Task Force
G-7	Group of Seven countries (Canada, France, Germany, Italy, Japan, the United Kingdom, and the United States)
GDP	gross domestic product
GED	Georeferenced Event Dataset
GTD	Global Terrorism Database
IBC	Iraq Body Count
IEP	Institute for Economics and Peace
ILO	International Labour Organization
IMB	International Maritime Bureau
IMF	International Monetary Fund
INSEC	Informal Sector Service Centre
LMPS	London Metropolitan Police Service

MIKE	Monitoring the Illegal Killing of Elephants
NCTC	National Counterterrorism Center (United States)
ODA	official development assistance
OECD	Organisation for Economic Co-operation and Development
PRIO	Peace Research Institute Oslo
SCAD	Social Conflict Analysis Database
SIGACTs	United States Central Command Significant Activities
TOC	transnational organized crime
UCDP	Uppsala Conflict Data Program
UN	United Nations
UNHCR	United Nations High Commissioner for Refugees
UNODC	United Nations Office on Drugs and Crime
VDC	Violations Documentation Center (Syria)
WITS	Worldwide Incidents Tracking System
WL	Wikileaks Iraq War Logs
World WISE	World Wildlife Seizures (database)

Overview

As world economies become ever more integrated, the flows of goods and services, people, and ideas have increased dramatically. At the same time, conflict, crime, and violence are also becoming more international in their scope, causes, and impact. The objective of this report, therefore, is to document how countries have a growing stake in each other's fate. Political and social stability and a country's ability to enforce the rule of law have implications not only for that country's neighbors but also beyond them. Each country's socio-politico-economic condition is subject to events taking place and policies adopted outside its borders.

Chapter 1 of this report assesses the extent to which conflict, crime, and violence have become regional or global problems because of the cross-border spillovers they generate. It documents several dimensions of such internationalization in many different domains. The main concern of the chapter is events that are closely associated with violence, because those events incur the heaviest human, economic, and social costs. The analysis covers intrastate conflicts, terrorism, and transnational crimes like piracy, human trafficking, and trade in illicit drugs and wildlife products. Discussion is restricted to criminal activities associated with violence broadly defined, setting aside such white-collar crimes as counterfeiting and cybercrimes. Interstate conflicts, which are essentially transnational, are not included in the analysis mainly because their resolution goes beyond finding appropriate domestic policy tools, which this report focuses on; moreover, their incidence has decreased dramatically since World War II ended.

The evidence points to growing internationalization across all these domains. In 2017 armed conflicts resulted in almost 87,000 fatalities;[1] of these, internationalized state-based conflicts and multicountry nonstate and one-sided conflicts accounted for 79 percent.[2] That year, too, saw

1

almost 11,000 terrorist attacks including 579 transnational attacks, affecting 103 countries and claiming over 26,000 lives, inclusive of 2,500 casualties from transnational attacks.[3] In addition to the human toll and the economic cost borne by nations suffering from internal wars, those domestic conflicts affect other countries—violence disrupts regional and international trade, and refugee flows pose a challenge to host countries. The analysis of global refugee flows, which numbered as many as 20 million people in 2017,[4] finds that refugees fleeing their home countries are now less likely to flee to an adjacent country, are more likely to travel much farther away, and are dispersed across many more destination countries. In 2012–17, the average distance traveled by refugees was 60 percent farther than the distances traveled in 1987–91.[5]

Similarly, global exports of illicit drugs like opium and cocaine are at a 30-year high, with most production concentrated in a few countries, whereas consumption of these drugs is global. International Labour Organization estimates place the global victims of transnational human trafficking at 5.7 million (ILO 2017). Despite the collapse of Somali piracy after 2012, piracy in international waters is still at the same level as in 1995.[6] Elephant and rhinoceros killings are also far above the levels of the early 2000s because of persistent international demand for wildlife products.

Chapter 2 examines the extent to which the drivers of conflict, crime, and violence have also become internationalized. To understand the forces that work to dampen or heighten violence, a "contest success function" approach is formulated, which is general enough to address such phenomena as illegal markets, terrorism, and insurgency. The model involves two opposing parties that decide how much effort to devote to violence, on the basis of the expected costs and benefits of such investments. In doing so, each party takes into account the other party's decisions.

This simple theoretical framework identifies four risk factors related to conflict, crime, and violence: (1) the *opportunity cost* of participation in violence—how well participants would fare in alternative activities; (2) the *returns to violence*—how much the perpetrators expect to gain if their violent strategy succeeds; (3) *state capacity*, such as the extent of law enforcement or military deployment; and (4) *intrinsic (nonmonetary) benefits of participation*, such as the resolution of prior grievances. The chapter then reviews the empirical evidence, mostly from the fields of economics, political science, and criminology, on the transnational drivers of violence, taking into account the difficulties of constructing clear empirical proxies for the theoretical parameters of the model. In doing so, the chapter illuminates the forces at play when the evidence allows for disentangling the confounding factors.

Chapter 2 identifies four major transnational determinants of crime and conflict: (1) international demand and supply shocks for the major products a country produces; (2) foreign regulations (for example, on illicit goods and services) that affect returns to producers and consumers along the supply chain; (3) technology diffusion; and (4) "conflict contagion" through either flows of tangible resources across borders (arms, fighters, money) or flows of intangible resources (ideas, inspirations, grievances). The chapter documents considerable evidence that in recent years the first two determinants have been major drivers of conflict and crime, mainly by changing either the opportunity cost of participating in conflict or the returns to engaging in violence or criminal activity. Because of data limitations and the difficulties in measuring the other parameters of the theoretical framework, the evidence linking transnational factors to state capacity or grievances is more tenuous. Some evidence suggests that conflict in one country leads to a higher risk of conflict in a neighboring country, though this theory is subject to the empirical difficulty of disentangling such contagion effects from correlated economic, climate, or political factors that may affect several countries at the same time. Finally, the evidence on technology diffusion is relatively recent, though studies have found that information and communication technologies such as radio or social media can be very effective both in coordinating protests and in building trust (or mistrust).

Special attention is devoted to "intentional" transnational drivers of violence, namely policies of foreign countries that are designed to alter the domestic socio-politico-economic landscape. The main instruments discussed are foreign military interventions and development assistance, with a brief discussion about targeted economic sanctions and anti-money-laundering initiatives. The main implication of the empirical stock-taking exercise is that the impact of foreign interventions on violence is ambiguous and highly context-specific. Military interventions might increase the state's ability to control crime and insurgency but might also worsen popular attitudes toward the government. Similarly, foreign aid might increase livelihoods and thus provide youth with an alternative to violence, but its impact on citizen perceptions is ambiguous: it might aggravate the corruption of officials and support a strategy of buying "hearts and minds." More important, the change in the balance of power created by an inflow of military/police or development assistance is likely to generate a reaction from criminal gangs or insurgent groups that takes the form of retaliation and sabotage operations. Chapter 2 concludes by highlighting the need for more research on the complementarity between provision of aid and provision of security, stressing throughout the pivotal role of the community in driving security and aid outcomes.

Chapter 3 elaborates on the rationale for international support for domestic resolution and prevention of conflict, crime, and violence. The political science literature has focused on failures to peacefully resolve conflict because of bargaining inefficiencies. In some cases, a third party can restore efficiency and hence avoid the welfare-destroying use of violence. In addition, the internationalization of both the causes and consequences of violence means that national security needs now to be reconceptualized as a bilateral, multilateral, or even global public good, and that foreign actors and international institutions can have an important role in providing it.

Chapter 3 examines the challenges underlying the internationalization of conflict, crime, and violence prevention. It highlights some constraints inherent in the arm's-length relationship between international actors and a sovereign nation. In particular, asymmetric information between governments and foreign entities limits the ability of foreign interventions to alter government incentives. Moreover, the provision of a public good such as global security and the elimination of transnational organized crimes by multiple individual countries are fraught with collective action problems. For instance, the international community is confronted by the free-riding problem, in that no single country has an incentive to assist a fragile state unless it has some stake in it. The evidence is clear that aid flows have been driven by donor geopolitical interests as well as recipient need. This chapter's original analysis of the drivers of foreign military interventions in intrastate conflicts finds that geopolitical considerations (for example, support on other issues, or overall alignment with the United States) and domestic political economy concerns play an important role in determining the likelihood that a given country will intervene in another country's conflict, even after controlling for prior links via trade, culture, or colonial ties. Although recognizing the possibility of competing interests between nations permeating global or multilateral institutions, the chapter argues that delegation of part of a country's foreign policy to international organizations can be one response to the collective action problem.

The report concludes with a call for more systematic effort to collect data on conflict, crime, and violence, which is critical for policy and research analyses. The methodological and technical difficulties with gathering information in fragile and conflict settings and on illegal activities are formidable, require appropriate resources, and involve the use of innovative tools in both collection and processing of data.

Furthermore, despite existing scope for foreign interventions to assist countries in meeting their stability and security challenges, the evidence collated in this report highlights the challenges associated with upholding the "do-no-harm" principle. In addition to the oft-discussed aid dependency risk, whereby foreign aid might worsen outcomes by crowding out government and private investments, foreign interventions have been documented to exacerbate fragility in some already volatile situations by affecting the stakes of engaging in violence.

In an increasingly interconnected world, moreover, policies in one country have implications for the level of conflict, crime, and violence beyond that country's borders—giving a transnational dimension to the "do-no-harm" principle. Finally, as countries increasingly become stakeholders in one another's fate, this report argues the need for more policy and financial instruments and institutions to move the settlement of disputes away from battlefields and toward national, regional, or international forums.

Notes

1. Estimates based on data from the Uppsala Conflict Data Program/Peace Research Institute Oslo (UCDP/PRIO) Armed Conflict Dataset, version 19.1, https://www.prio.org/Data/Armed-Conflict/UCDP-PRIO.
2. Estimates based on data from the UCDP/PRIO Armed Conflict Dataset, version 19.1, https://www.prio.org/Data/Armed-Conflict/UCDP-PRIO.
3. Estimates based on data from the Global Terrorism Database, http://www.start-dev.umd.edu/gtd.
4. Estimates based on data from the United Nations High Commissioner for Refugees' Population Statistics Database, http://popstats.unhcr.org/en/overview.
5. Estimates based on data from the United Nations High Commissioner for Refugees' Population Statistics Database, http://popstats.unhcr.org/en/overview.
6. Estimates based on data from the International Maritime Bureau Piracy Reporting Centre Database, https://www.icc-ccs.org/piracy-reporting-centre.

Reference

ILO (International Labour Organization). 2017. *Global Estimates of Modern Slavery: Forced Labour and Forced Marriage*. Geneva: ILO.

CHAPTER 1

Crime, Conflict, and Violence without Borders

Like so many other aspects of human experience, conflict, crime, and violence have become globalized. This report documents the growing internationalization of violent events like civil wars, acts of terrorism, and organized crime. Civil wars today reverberate beyond the confines of national boundaries, and the first two decades of this century have seen a rise in intrastate conflicts that take place across or involve numerous countries. The consequences of these conflicts are also being experienced farther afield, with refugees traveling farther from their home countries than ever before. More terror attacks are now transnational than at any point since 1970. The reach of criminal organizations extends across regions, and continued demand for wildlife products threatens the survival of many endangered species. Countries are now producing and trafficking more illicit drugs, such as opium from Afghanistan and cocaine from Colombia, than at any point since the United Nations Office on Drugs and Crime (UNODC) began collecting data. Although international efforts to counter maritime piracy along the Somali coast have been effective, piracy persists in Southeast Asia and in the Gulf of Guinea. The International Labour Organization (ILO) estimates the number of global victims of transnational human trafficking at 5.7 million (ILO 2017). These headline trends reflect the limited ability of local governments to curtail the prevalence of conflict, crime, and violence.

This report examines a wide range of data sources to document the extent to which conflict, crime, and violence have been internationalized. In this context, "internationalized" means that a country experiences the consequences of such events taking place in a different country, or that the drivers of conflict and crime emanate from a different country. The term "transnational" crime or conflict refers to either of these effects. In looking at crime, the report narrows its focus to criminal activities that have major cross-border implications and are associated with physical violence. It is thus relevant to examine crimes like terrorism and piracy on the high seas, and illegal markets for, among others, human trafficking, illicit drugs, and wildlife trade. The analysis does not cover capital-intensive crimes—such as white-collar crimes, counterfeiting, and cybercrimes—but focuses instead on labor-intensive crimes. The report discusses trends in armed conflict, terrorism, and transnational trade in illicit goods and services, even though, because these activities are illegal, relevant data are scarce. Finally, because intra- and interstate conflicts differ in their drivers and in the policy instruments to mitigate them, the report restricts analysis of violent civil conflicts to civil wars, especially given the urgency created by their increased incidence, even as violent interstate conflicts have become rarer.

Armed conflict

This report's analysis of global conflict relies on databases from the Uppsala Conflict Data Program (UCDP). UCDP defines an armed conflict as an organized actor (state or nonstate) using armed force against another orga-nized actor or against civilians and that violence resulting in at least one direct death. The analysis therefore excludes political protests that are not accompanied by fatal violence. Conflicts are recorded as either state-based (with a government as one of the parties), non-state-based (conflicts between rebel groups and militias or between informally organized groups such as ethnic or religious groups), or one-sided (involving the targeted killing of unarmed civilians by states or formally organized nonstate groups). These categories allow for the examination of the full spectrum of armed conflicts affecting the world. Box 1.1 evaluates the datasets on armed conflicts.

After a decade of relatively low conflict intensity, there has been a resur-gence in conflicts and fatalities. Globally, in 2017, armed conflicts resulted in almost 87,000 fatalities. Although this number is down from 2014, when almost 130,000 deaths were recorded, it is still much higher than in the previous decade (2001–10) when deaths averaged 33,000 a year. Even in terms of global population figures, global fatalities from armed conflicts reached 1.8 deaths per 100,000 inhabitants in 2014—a threefold increase over the 2001–10 average. The continuing conflicts in the Syrian Arab Republic and Iraq are a significant factor; between 2012 and 2017 those

Box 1.1 The gaps and data limitations of datasets on armed conflicts

Systematic collection of data has resulted in a proliferation of datasets on conflict. Beginning with the Correlates of War (CoW) data project, the most common measure of conflict intensity has been the number of battlefield-related deaths (BRDs). Proponents, such as Singer and Small (1982, 206), argue that war must be defined in terms of violence, not only because "war is impossible without violence" but also because the "taking of human life [is] the primary and dominant characteristic of war." Researchers have therefore adopted BRDs as a proxy for conflict intensity. Since then, more datasets tracking global conflict fatalities have been established, notably the Uppsala Conflict Data Program (UCDP) and the Armed Conflict Location & Event Data Project (ACLED). Simultaneously, the number of datasets for specific countries has increased (SIGACTs for Afghanistan and Iraq, CERAC for Colombia, INSEC for Nepal, BFRS for Pakistan, and VDC for the Syrian Arab Republic are a few examples[a]). Even among these datasets, fatalities have been the predominant measure of conflict. Ansorg, Haas, and Strasheim (2013) systematically reviewed over 257 databases on the nexus of conflict, security, and institutions. They found that, of these databases, 179 have global coverage (except for countries with fewer than 500,000 inhabitants) whereas the rest focus on individual countries and regions.

Despite their proliferation in recent years, many datasets on conflict still have methodological shortcomings. Most datasets recording global conflicts define a threshold of fatalities for inclusion. These criteria vary across datasets and in some cases over years. The CoW database, for example, has the highest threshold for inclusion (1,000 BRDs/year). Its methodology for inclusion, however, has "changed at least three times" between its inception in 1972 and 2004 (Sambanis 2004, 817) and once

since 2010. At first, CoW did not have an explicit cutoff. A cutoff was introduced in the 1984 iteration and then relaxed for "extrasystemic" wars in 1994 and for "extrastate" wars in 2001 (Sambanis 2004). This discrepancy makes it particularly difficult to compare conflicts. For example, the Basque and the Northern Ireland conflicts are still not included because they do not meet the strict threshold maintained for intrastate conflicts (Gleditsch et al. 2002). In an analytical exercise using CoW data, intrastate conflicts would thus appear to be less frequent than extrastate conflicts due to a heterogeneous application of the cutoff threshold. The threshold for inclusion in the UCDP/PRIO [Peace Research Institute Oslo] Dataset, by comparison, is 25 BRDs/year. This threshold allows for a richer coverage of civil conflicts (defined as conflicts with fatalities ranging between 25 and 1,000 per year) as well as civil wars (with over 1,000 recorded BRDs/year), improving its usefulness in analytical exercises. ACLED, in contrast, adds nonviolent events that take place on the sidelines of conflicts, such as protests and riots that do not result in casualties. Ansorg, Haas, and Strasheim (2013) provide an additional example of a nonstate conflict dataset that captures conflicts below the 25 BRDs threshold—the Social Conflict in Africa Database, later renamed the Social Conflict Analysis Database (SCAD).

Temporal and spatial coverage of the data is also a methodological problem for researchers. Although the CoW database has the longest coverage of any conflict database (currently the years 1816–2007), researchers have argued against the usefulness of pre–World War II observations in studying contemporary conflicts (Gleditsch et al. 2002). The UCDP provides multiple datasets ranging from a shorter but more extensive georeferenced event dataset covering the 28-year period of 1989–2017

(continued)

Box 1.1 continued

to a longer but less granular dataset for 1946–2012. ACLED has the fastest turnaround time for coding new conflict events (the most recent data are for November 2019), but it also suffers from having the shortest time coverage, with most African conflicts dating back only to 1997, Asian conflicts to 2010, and conflicts within the Middle East and North Africa region starting only in 2016.

These differences in set construction can affect the results of empirical analysis. Eck (2012), having found more coding errors in the ACLED data, warns that the dataset may not be able to capture subnational patterns effectively because of uneven quality control. She argues that UCDP has limited coverage because it does not include nonviolent events such as protest and troop movements, both of which issues can bias findings. To counteract this limitation, researchers continually advise combining multiple datasets such as those georeferencing terrorism and organized conflict event data (Findley and Young 2012), matching terrorism events to armed groups (Fortna 2015; Polo and Gleditsch 2016), and matching events recorded in the Global Terrorism Database (GTD) to perpetrators from the Big, Allied, and Dangerous (BAAD) dataset (this report) and the ACLED, UCDP, the GTD, and the SCAD in order to develop a fuller coverage of events (Donnay et al. 2018).

An almost universal reliance on media reports as sources of information introduces additional bias. Most conflict databases rely on news reports for information on conflict events. Notable exceptions are databases that rely on information obtained directly from military authorities (see Weidmann's [2015] review of the SIGACTs database in Afghanistan) or police departments (Draca, Machin, and Witt [2011] use data from the London Metropolitan Police Service [LMPS]). Carpenter, Fuller, and Roberts (2013), testing the relative coverage of conflict events between the Wikileaks Iraq War Logs (WL) and the Iraq Body Count (IBC) datasets, found that 94 percent of events with over 20 fatalities were in both datasets, compared to only 17 percent of those with fewer fatalities. Weidmann (2015) found comparable results after comparing the coverage of conflicts by the Afghan War Diary and ACLED. Similar disparities are found for events in urban areas (Kalyvas 2004) and especially the capital (Bocquier and Maupeu 2005) as well as in countries with more authoritarian regimes (Baum and Zhukov 2015; Drakos and Gofas 2006) and countries on opposite sides of conflicts (Zhukov and Baum 2016). Rohner and Frey (2007) and Asal and Hoffman (2016) found that the choice of terrorist attack may in fact be endogenous to the ability and ease of access for media outlets. New research by Rød and Weidmann (2015) and Weidmann (2016) found that the spread of telephone coverage can greatly equalize this disparity.

a. BFRS = Bueno de Mesquita, Fair, Rais, and Shapiro Political Violence in Pakistan dataset; CERAC = Conflict Analysis Resource Center Database of the Armed Conflict in Colombia; INSEC = Informal Sector Service Centre Human Rights Yearbooks; SIGACTs = United States Central Command Significant Activities data; VDC = Violations Documentation Center in Syria database.

conflicts were responsible for almost 350,000 fatalities. An interesting point to note from the UCDP data is that, although nonstate conflicts are now the most prevalent form of armed conflict (figure 1.1, panel a), most deaths continue to occur in state-based conflicts (figure 1.1, panel b). The conflicts within Syria headline this trend; however, even after removing Syria from the analysis, the upward trend does not disappear.

Figure 1.1 Armed conflicts: Incidence and fatalities, by type, 1989–2017

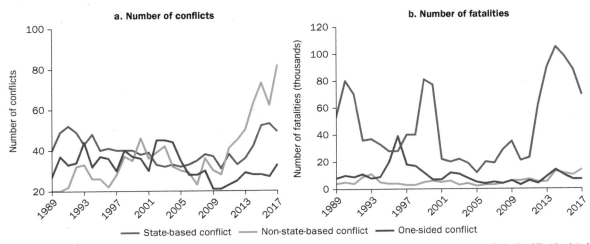

Sources: Uppsala Conflict Data Program (UCDP) Battle-Related Deaths Dataset, version 19.1, https://ucdp.uu.se/downloads/index.html#battlerelated; UCDP One-Sided Violence Dataset, version 19.1, https://ucdp.uu.se/downloads/index.html#onesided; UCDP Non-State Conflict Dataset, version 19.1, https://ucdp.uu.se/downloads/index.html#nonstate.

Note: Panel b excludes 1994 Rwandan genocide statistics.

Figure 1.2 State-based armed conflicts, by type, 1946–2017

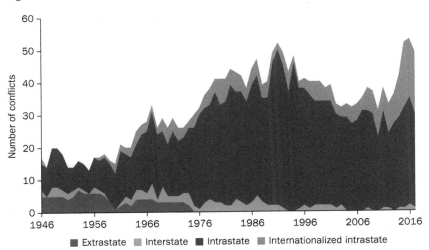

Source: Uppsala Conflict Data Program/Peace Research Institute Oslo Armed Conflict Dataset, version 19.1, https://www.prio.org/Data/Armed-Conflict/UCDP-PRIO/.

Many state-based armed conflicts are now international. Almost 40 percent of those taking place in 2017 involved interventions from third-party governments. Figure 1.2 illustrates the increase in the number of internationalized intrastate conflicts over the past decade. Despite a reduction in the number of interstate conflicts, the incidence of intrastate conflicts has remained relatively stable over this period. Additionally, extrasystemic (extrastate) conflicts took place between a state and a nonstate group outside its own territory, but the last of these colonial conflicts ended in 1974. Taking this longer view, the analysis finds that fatalities from state-based armed conflicts have experienced a strong decline since the end of the Second World War. Although a lack of pre-1989 data on nonstate and one-sided civil conflicts restricts a fuller analysis of historical conflict patterns, overall, fatalities associated with state-based armed conflicts have dropped significantly since the end of the Second World War (World Bank 2011). As in figure 1.3, which shows how the Syrian Civil War drives the uptake in fatalities associated with armed conflicts, much of the historical peaks in state-based armed conflicts were driven by five conflicts: the Chinese Civil War (1946–50), the Korean War (1950–53), the Vietnam War (1965–75), the Iran–Iraq War (1980–88), and the Soviet–Afghan War (1978–89). These five conflicts account for almost 60 percent of all battle-related fatalities recorded between 1946 and 2008.[1]

About 155 conflicts (nonstate and one-sided) have taken place across several countries. These multicountry conflicts originate in a single country and spread to other countries either through isolated transnational attacks by nonstate actors or through an expansion of the area of conflict. Combined, these internationalized state-based conflicts and multicountry nonstate and one-sided conflicts accounted for 79 percent

Figure 1.3 All armed conflicts, by type, 1989–2017

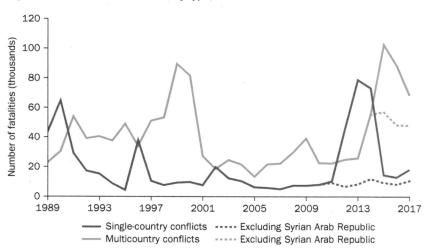

Source: Uppsala Conflict Data Program Georeferenced Event Dataset (GED) Global, version 19.1, https://ucdp.uu.se/downloads/index.html#ged_global.

of all fatalities (68,000) in 2017. Even excluding the Syrian conflict, almost 48,000 fatalities were associated with internationalized intrastate and multicountry conflicts (figure 1.3).

Armed conflicts impose costs on countries affected by disruption of their economies, institutions, and societies. Although it is difficult to fully account for the costs associated with armed conflicts, estimates from the Institute for Economics and Peace (IEP) placed the economic cost of conflicts in 2017 at a trillion dollars based on the direct loss of life, the impact on local economies, and the costs associated with the displacement of people (IEP 2018).[2] Since 2011, the continuing civil wars and insurgencies in the Middle East, North Africa, and South Asia have pushed up the costs associated with armed conflicts by almost 93 percent. Nowhere is this more evident than in Syria, where, over the course of six years, 295,000 casualties have been reported, 6 million people displaced at home and abroad, and almost 27 percent of the entire housing stock destroyed or damaged, resulting between 2011 and 2016 in a cumulative loss of US$226 billion—about 400 percent of the country's 2010 preconflict gross domestic product (GDP) (World Bank 2017).

The negative effects of armed conflicts are experienced in other countries besides those where conflicts are taking place. Like the IEP study, Alamir et al. (2018) found that, if there had been no armed conflicts between 1960 and 2014, global GDP in real terms would have been US$26.8 trillion higher in 2014 (equivalent to 33 percent of global GDP). Notably, they also found that costs from neighboring conflicts were almost as high as costs from domestic conflicts. The negative impacts of neighboring conflicts on domestic economic growth (De Groot 2010; Murdoch and Sandler 2002, 2004) and bilateral trade (Bayer and Rupert 2004; Glick and Taylor 2010; Martin, Mayer, and Thoenig 2008a, 2008b) are well-documented.

Population displacements are another transnational consequence of armed conflicts. Since 2000, the population displaced globally has more than doubled. Although many countries have long experienced displacement crises, the increase in refugee flows to Europe since 2010 has focused the attention of policy makers and the general public on this question. For much of the analysis, this report focuses on data on globally displaced populations since the 1980s because data before then likely exhibit gaps, specifically, relating to internally displaced people in many decolonized nations. As of 2017, more than 68.9 million individuals were forcibly displaced by persecution, conflict, generalized violence, or human rights violations: of these individuals, 20 million people were refugees in foreign countries.[3]

Figure 1.4 Global refugee population, 1951–2017

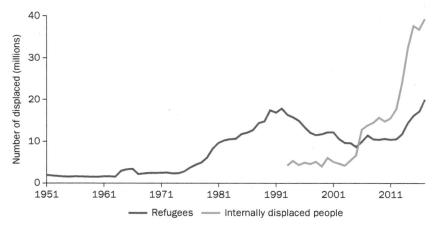

Source: United Nations High Commissioner for Refugees Population Statistics Database, http://popstats
.unhcr.org/en/overview.

Figure 1.4 charts the increase in the global refugee population since 1975, and the steep increase in the number of refugees over the past decade is clear. At the same time, however, twice as many people are displaced within their own national borders. Such refugee movements can impose significant costs on destination countries. Ferris and Kirişci (2016) estimated the total cost of hosting Syrian refugees through 2016 at US$8 billion for Turkey, US$4.5 billion for Jordan, and US$4 billion for Lebanon.

This report examined whether the dynamics of refugee flows in conflicts have changed in recent years. To do so, the analysis assembled data on worldwide bilateral refugee flows, conflicts, and geography and used a model borrowed from trade economics that predicts bilateral trade flows on the basis of country size and distance between two countries. This "gravity" model is used to explain refugee flows between two countries according to the distance between them, whether they share a border, and whether they have a common language (for details, see Devictor et al. 2019, summarized in annex 1A).

The main finding from the analysis is that, once they decide to flee their home country, refugees are now likely to travel much farther, are less likely to settle in an adjacent country, and are spread more evenly across more destination countries. These findings imply that refugee flows have an extended global reach. Data on refugees for this report come from the United Nations High Commissioner for Refugees (UNHCR), which provides only statistics on the number of refugees but does not allow for accounting for changes in the composition of refugee source countries. For instance, if conflicts that give rise to refugee flows over time occurred in more-remote countries, the distance traveled would increase—not because it is now easier for refugees to travel farther but because of changes in the geography of conflict. To rule out pure compositional changes, the analysis looks at changes within countries and over time. Figure 1.5 plots the time effects for the average distance traveled, with 95 percent confidence intervals. The coefficients can be interpreted as the percentage increase in the average distance traveled by a refugee in a given period relative to the benchmark period, which is the first five years of data (1987–91). The increase in the average distance traveled, conditional on source country fixed effects, is apparent. Relative to the first reference period, distances traveled by refugees have risen over time, and the differences are statistically significant. For 2012–17, the average distance traveled by refugees was 60 percent higher than the distances traveled in 1987–91.

A related finding is that the share of refugees going to a contiguous country has been dropping (see figure 1.6). Here, the outcome variable is a share, and thus the coefficients should be interpreted as an absolute change in the share—that is, –0.1 means that share fell from, say, 80 percent to 70 percent. Once again, conditional on the country fixed effect, the drop in the share of refugees going to a contiguous country is clear. The coefficient estimates are

Figure 1.5   Average distance traveled by a refugee, 1987–2017

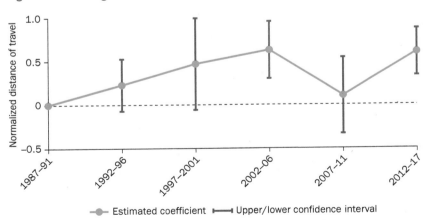

Source: United Nations High Commissioner for Refugees Population Statistics Database, http://popstats .unhcr.org/en/overview.

Note: The decrease in distance traveled for the period 2007-11 is likely attributable to the 2008 financial crisis that slowed down flows to Organisation for Economic Co-operation and Development countries.

Figure 1.6 Share of refugees going to a contiguous country, 1987–2017

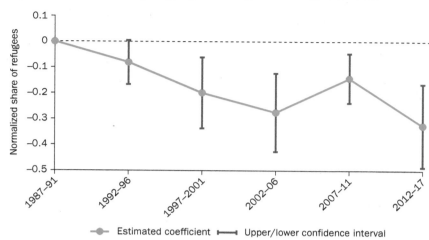

Source: United Nations High Commissioner for Refugees Population Statistics Database, http://popstats.unhcr.org/en/overview.

large: comparing late in the period to the beginning, the share going to a contiguous country has fallen by as much as 30 percentage points.

Here again, the downward trend is interrupted during the financial crisis years of 2007–11. Another manifestation of the wider geographical reach of refugees is the greater number of destination countries. To document the diversity of destinations over time, the analysis computes an index for the relative concentration (Herfindahl index) of refugee shares going to each destination from each source country in each time period and takes the average across countries in each time period.[4] There is a clear downward trend in the Herfindahl index, implying greater diversification of refugee flows across locations (see figure 1.7). Refugees from conflict are also participating more in "secondary" movements; upon finding a place to settle after leaving their home countries, many attempt to migrate even farther, often to Organisation for Economic Co-operation and Development (OECD) countries (World Bank 2018). The best-known examples are the refugee flows from other Latin American countries into Mexico and then into the United States, and from Middle Eastern countries into Turkey and then the European Union through Greece and Italy. Often, the destination countries bear the costs of hosting refugees.

The findings imply that wealthy countries are now more affected by the pressures of refugee inflows than they were in the past. In the early 1990s, just 10 percent of refugees ended up in a high-income OECD country.

Figure 1.7   Mean Herfindahl index of destinations, five-year moving average, 1991–2017

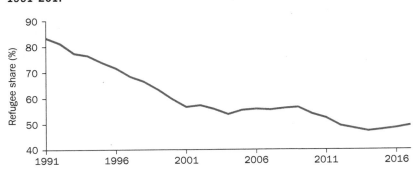

Source: United Nations High Commissioner for Refugees Population Statistics Database, http://popstats .unhcr.org/en/overview.

By the mid-2000s, the share had grown to nearly 35 percent; after falling somewhat, the share in the most recent period is above 20 percent—double the value in the early 1990s. The pattern for refugees coming to Europe is even more pronounced: with some fluctuations in the interim, at the beginning of the 1990s only about 10 percent of refugees ended up in Europe; however, the most recent data give that share as 40 percent.

Although the spillovers of civil wars have been spreading geographically, a growing concern is that climate change will exacerbate conflict and social tensions, which would intensify global exposure to national civil wars. According to a report commissioned by the G-7,[5] climate change worsens fragility and promotes violent conflict (Rüttinger et al. 2015) because it can intensify local competition for scarce resources, price volatility, livelihood insecurity, forced migration, and tensions in international resource management.

Numerous empirical studies have established a strong link between climate shocks and conflict. In an early paper, Miguel, Satyanath, and Sergenti (2004) found that between 1981 and 1999 lower rainfall led to more conflict in a panel of 41 Sub-Saharan countries. Similarly, Burke et al. (2009) found a link between higher temperatures and the likelihood of conflict in Africa. In a metaanalysis, Hsiang, Burke, and Miguel (2013) examined 60 papers on the relationship between climate shocks (measured by variations in temperature and precipitation) and conflict. These studies relied on either natural experiments or quasi-experiments or were reevaluated using consistent methodologies. The analysts found that a one-standard-deviation change in climate (warmer temperatures or more extreme rainfall) increased interpersonal violence by 4 percent and intergroup conflict by 14 percent.[6]

A subnational link between climate and conflict has also been identified. For instance, using spatial analysis in a granular small-grid dataset of conflicts in Africa, Harari and La Ferrara (2018) found that climate shocks during the local growing season persistently affect the incidence of conflict, and also generate negative spillovers to neighboring areas. Behind this evidence of the short-term effect, multiple mechanisms could be at play. Some studies suggest that the effects of climate shocks on conflict arise primarily from a decline in economic opportunities (see Dell, Jones, and Olken 2014 for a review of the literature).[7]

Transnational terrorism

There is no universally accepted definition of terrorism. The US State Department defines it as "premeditated, politically motivated violence perpetrated against noncombatant targets by subnational groups or clandestine agents. (As per 22 USCS 2656f)." The Global Terrorism Database (GTD), maintained by the University of Maryland, defines it as "the threatened or actual use of illegal force and violence by a non-state actor to attain a political, economic, religious, or social goal through fear, coercion, or intimidation."[8] Although the use of violence and the political motivations for it are inherent to the term's definition, what makes a use illegal or a target a noncombatant is largely left to interpretation. The difficulty in defining the term "terrorism" is epitomized by the cliché "one person's terrorist is another's freedom fighter." Without delving too deeply into this definitional quagmire, this report refrains from narrowly defining terrorism. Instead it leverages the work already undertaken by GTD authors, which forms the basis of much of the current analysis: "In the absence of a universally accepted definition of terrorism, GTD uses several coded criteria to cover a broad range of definitions of terrorism through a combination of inclusiveness and filtering."[9]

By definition, some overlap exists between events identified as acts of terror listed in the GTD and armed conflicts listed by the UCDP. Specifically, use of violence against civilians by nonstate actors is included in both. The GTD, however, excludes attacks on civilians by state actors (also known as state-sponsored acts of terrorism) whereas the UCDP lists them as one-sided conflict events. Conversely, the UCDP does not count acts of terror that do not conform to a larger armed conflict involving either a state or a nonstate actor, but the GTD does. Another important distinction is that, although the GTD codes eight types of events—among them assassinations, bombings, hijackings, and kidnappings—data on armed conflicts exclude events that do not result in any casualties. Anderton and Carter (2011) provide an extensive comparison of conflict and terrorism datasets.[10]

Over the past few years, incidents of terrorism have spiked. In 2017, almost 11,000 terrorist events claimed over 26,000 lives (figure 1.8, panel a). Like armed conflicts, the number of attacks and fatalities is considerably higher since 2005 than it was before, though there has been

Figure 1.8 Terrorist attacks and fatalities worldwide, 1970–2017

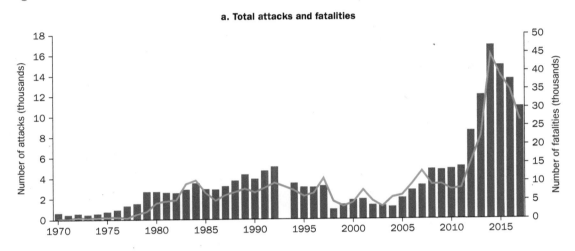

a. Total attacks and fatalities

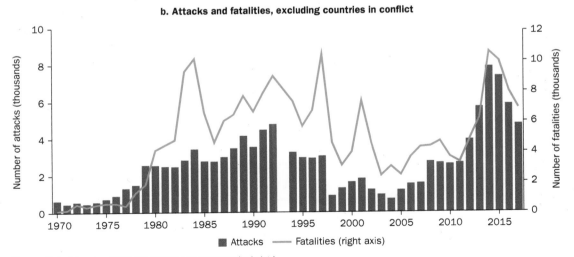

b. Attacks and fatalities, excluding countries in conflict

■ Attacks ── Fatalities (right axis)

Source: Global Terrorism Database, https://www.start.umd.edu/gtd.

Note: Data not available for 1993. Panel b excludes attacks and fatalities in Afghanistan, Iraq, Nigeria, the Philippines, Somalia, the Syrian Arab Republic, and the Republic of Yemen.

a decline since 2014. In 2017, 102 countries experienced individual attacks, but most of those attacks were in countries also experiencing armed conflicts. Among these, Iraq has witnessed an average of 1,740 attacks each year since 2004, more than any other country except Pakistan, which suffered more attacks in 2012. This again points to the overlap between acts of terrorism and the presence of civil war. Of the 10 countries that experienced the highest number of terrorism attacks, 7 were also experiencing civil war in 2017. These 7 countries (Afghanistan, Iraq, Nigeria, the Philippines, Somalia, Syria, and the Republic of Yemen) accounted for 56 percent of all terrorist attacks and 74 percent of terrorism fatalities in 2017. Excluding these countries, however, does not eliminate the spike that has been witnessed in the number of attacks taking place since 2014 but does make the number more comparable to levels experienced previously in the 1980s and early 1990s (figure 1.8, panel b).

To focus on transnationality, the analysis identified attacks where the groups responsible were located outside the country in which the attack took place. Nearly half of the incidents in the GTD cannot be attributed to any group because of a lack of information. For the rest, the GTD codes the names of groups that claimed responsibility for the attack. This analysis matched individual groups identified with the country of origin of 513 of the most active groups identified in the Big, Allied, and Dangerous (BAAD) version 2.0 dataset.[11] This matching was further extended to 797 individual groups that were responsible for almost 90,000 events.[12] The analysis thus attempted to split attacks that originate from groups based within the country and from groups outside.

Incidents of transnational terrorism—groups claiming responsibility located in a country different from where attacks took place—have gone up significantly since 2010 (figure 1.9), and the pattern of transnational events is similar to that for total attacks (figure 1.8). (This analysis comes with an obvious warning about data quality, in terms of both the universe of terrorism events and the truthfulness of groups claiming responsibility.) As of 2017, transnational incidents account for 14 percent of all identified events and 19 percent of all the casualties.[13] In 2017, 46 countries suffered from transnational attacks. An obvious question that arises from this finding is whether today's terrorist groups are becoming increasingly international in nature (with local affiliates across nations) or their reach is becoming more global (as in the illustrative case of the 9/11 hijackers). Unfortunately, the quality of data does not allow for a response to this question—partly because it is not possible to distinguish the links of patronage between terror groups as either totemic or operational networks. Additionally, because of their

Figure 1.9 Transnational terrorist attacks and fatalities, 1970–2017

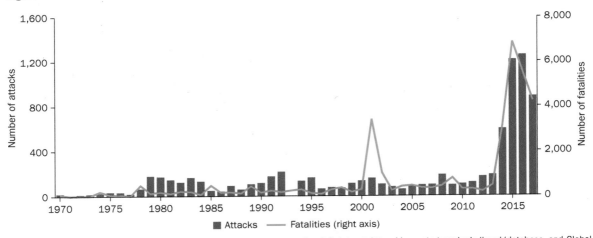

Sources: World Bank analysis based on the Big, Allied, and Dangerous version 2.0 dataset, https://www.start.umd.edu/baad/database, and Global Terrorism Database (GTD), https://start.umd.edu/data-tools/global-terrorism-database-gtd.

Note: Data not available for 1993.

unstable nature, groups splinter, merge, or otherwise rename themselves, all of which actions remain untracked in the data.

In addition to their human costs, terrorist attacks have economic costs. Although an accurate assessment of the complete economic impact of any attack is difficult, the IEP estimates the costs to be US$52 billion for 2017 (50 percent lower since 2014, but 500 percent higher than in 2000) (IEP 2018). A European Parliament study found that, between 2004 and 2016, Europe lost €185 billion of growth to terrorism, of which €5.6 billion was in direct losses from fatalities, injuries, and damages to infrastructure (van Ballegooij and Bakowski 2018).

Illicit markets

The current unprecedented openness in trade, finance, travel, and communication has allowed illicit markets to grow beyond the confines of any one jurisdiction. Among illicit activities are the production and trafficking of narcotics, human trafficking, the trafficking of illegal wildlife products, maritime piracy, and small arms trafficking. The UNODC terms these activities as transnational organized crimes (TOCs). Because they are illicit, no quality data are available on their scale and reach. There is only a collection of estimates of the prevalence and magnitude of activities and markets based on remote monitoring, qualitative surveys, and

Table 1.1   Global proceeds from transnational organized criminal networks

Transnational criminal market	Proceeds (US$, billion)	Share of proceeds trafficked across borders (percent)
Drugs	320	50
Counterfeiting	250	40
Human trafficking	31.6	43
Wildlife	7.8–10.0	Not available
Timber	7	Not available
Fish	4.2–9.5	Not available
Art and cultural property	3.4–6.3	Not available
Gold	2.3	Not available
Human organs	0.6–1.2	Not available
Small arms and light weapons	0.3–1.0	Not available
Diamonds and colored gemstones	0.9	Not available
Total (midpoint estimates)	**~645**	

Source: UNODC 2011a.

a host of proxy indicators. The lack of good data makes it difficult for law-enforcement agencies to detect and prevent these activities, and it also makes robust empirical analysis difficult.

A UNODC (2011a) study estimates that roughly US$645 billion are generated from various transnational criminal markets (table 1.1). Of this total, the proceeds of TOC networks—including drug trafficking, counterfeiting, human trafficking, and arms smuggling—are estimated to be as high as 1.5 percent of global GDP in 2009, or roughly US$870 billion (UNODC 2011a). Assuming these proportions have remained unchanged, this corresponding estimate would place the value of global TOC at US$1.3 trillion in 2018. Because this study particularly focuses on the intersection of crime, conflict, and violence in an internationalized world, it restricts its attention to a few key—illustrative—illicit markets that either are essentially transnational in nature or employ violence in their production or the trafficking channels.

Drug trafficking

Psychoactive drugs like cocaine or heroin are almost universally prohibited. Yet an estimated 275 million people (1 in 18 adults throughout the world) used an illegal drug in 2016 (UNODC 2018a). These rates have been rising steadily: in 2016 almost 20 million more people used drugs than in 2015, an increase of 7.8 percent. With over 192 million users in 2016, cannabis continues to be the most abused narcotic in the world. It also enjoys a ubiquitous level of cultivation (135 countries reported cultivation of marijuana to the UNODC in 2016) and consumption (146 national customs offices reported seizing some marijuana in 2016).

The illicit drug market, especially for narcotics like cocaine and heroin, has an important cross-border dimension. The base plants for these drugs, coca and poppy, are cultivated in only a few countries, but demand is global: between 2010 and 2015, 153 countries reported cocaine seizures to the UNODC (2018a). Higher production of these commodities necessarily implies higher illicit transnational trade. Coca, the plant base for cocaine, is mainly grown in the Andes in South America, in Bolivia, Colombia, and Peru. Similarly, the world's supply of opium/heroin is sourced almost entirely from poppies cultivated in Afghanistan and Myanmar. The UNODC has for more than three decades published the Illicit Crop Monitoring Reports on cultivation of coca and poppy and production of cocaine and opium. In figure 1.10, panel a shows the cultivation of coca and poppy since 1986. Although the total area under coca cultivation fell between 1989 and 2013, it has since more than doubled. Poppy cultivation rose almost 200 percent between 2001 and 2017. Panel b of figure 1.10 shows estimates of production of cocaine and opium from the base commodities. In 2017, Afghanistan produced 86 percent of the world's supply of opium and Colombia 84 percent of the world's cocaine supply. In both cases, the production of opium and cocaine is outpacing the increase in global population but not of real GDP.

Figure 1.10 Cultivation and production of illicit narcotics, 1986–2017

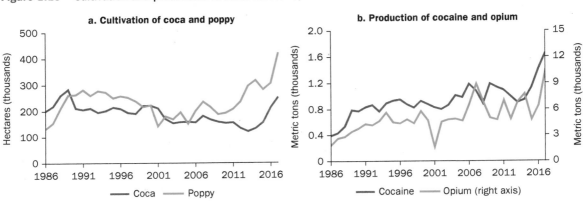

Source: UNODC 2019.

Violence often accompanies transnational trade in illicit commodities. It has been argued that higher prices resulting from criminalization of narcotics heightens the economic incentives for drug traffickers to operate, resulting in more violence, corruption, and political instability (World Bank 2010). Because it prevents traffickers from using legal and judicial systems, prohibition has instead provided incentives for the use of violence (Miron and Zwiebel 1995). As a result, most of the 121,669 homicides reported in Mexico over 2006–12 have been attributed to drug trafficking (Calderón, Ferreira, and Shirk 2018). The total global drug trafficking market in 2014 was estimated to be worth US$426 billion to US$652 billion, over 22 percent of which was attributable to cocaine. The UNODC (2017) estimated that the Taliban raised nearly US$150 million from the opium trade in the form of taxes on production and extortion for financing of the insurgency in 2011, which corresponded to roughly 38 percent of the insurgents' total income (UNODC 2011b).

Human trafficking and the smuggling of migrants

The ILO (2017) estimates that one in four instances of human trafficking is transnational. Human trafficking covers recruitment, transportation, or receipt of persons either by coercion or abuse of vulnerability for the purpose of exploitation (UNODC 2018b). Among the many reasons for trafficking, to varying degrees, are sexual exploitation, forced labor, servitude, or the removal of organs. Some categories of human trafficking are more transnational than others; for instance, 74 percent of victims of forced sexual exploitation are likely to be taken across national borders (ILO 2017).

Data on detection of trafficking victims shows an upward trend since 2003. Because human trafficking is clandestine and traces of it are limited, tracking its actual incidence is difficult. The main sources of data on human trafficking are international organizations that collate data streams from national police and customs authorities. From these sources, it appears that worldwide the numbers of victims and cases of human trafficking reported per country have been going up (figure 1.11). Because the number of countries reporting trafficking statistics to the UNODC has been growing, however, the trend may simply reflect better coverage. When changes in the number of reporting countries are controlled for, the rise in human trafficking since 2010 is evident (figure 1.11). The increase in the number of victims may also be affected by changes in national enforcement capacity

Figure 1.11 **Trends in detection of human trafficking, 2003–16**

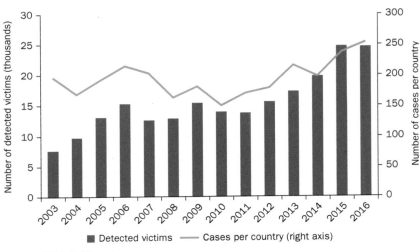

Source: UNODC 2018b.

to identify the crimes and in willingness to share the data (UNODC 2018b).[14] In particular, there has been a well-documented increase in international efforts with the issuance of UN protocols on human trafficking (OHCHR 2000a) and migrant smuggling (OHCHR 2000b), which spurred a rapid increase in the number of countries criminalizing human trafficking (UNODC 2018b).

The routes for transregional flows of human trafficking tend to track migration routes. Human trafficking and the smuggling of migrants are two very different concepts. Human trafficking victims are not always migrants (not necessarily crossing borders), and, unlike migration, of necessity human trafficking entails coercion. Migrant smuggling is a distinct transnational crime that involves payment, in cash or in kind, in exchange for facilitation of an illegal crossing into another country. Nevertheless, human trafficking and migration flows are sometimes connected. As for migrant smuggling, transregional flows tend to go from developing (Africa, South Asia, East Asia, and Latin America) to developed (North America, Europe, and Gulf countries) regions that offer more economic opportunities (UNODC 2016a). Furthermore, although migrant smuggling initially has the consent of migrants, it can ultimately entail such crimes as coercion, exploitation, fraud, or debt bondage. For example, on the basis of the 2016 European Asylum Seekers Survey, the World Bank (2018) has observed that 45 percent of the recent wave of African migrants coming to Europe through Libya suffered violence in transit, 11 percent worked without any compensation, and another 10 percent worked without receiving cash payments. Mahmoud and Trebesch (2010), using household surveys in certain Eastern European countries, also found that migrant families from high-migration areas are significantly more likely to have a trafficked victim among their members than families from low-migration regions.

Illegal migrants apprehended by authorities indicate a large influx into the European Union and the United States. Apprehensions of illegal migrants into the United States grew from fewer than 100,000 a year in the 1960s to more than 1.5 million in the late 1990s, though there has since been a progressive reduction. In 2015 the more recent migration crisis in Europe translated into more than 2 million illegal entries, up from an average annual flow of fewer than half a million. Although the data show only apprehensions, which can be affected by changes in enforcement capacity, they point to large flows of illegal migration into developed countries.

Wildlife trafficking

Much of the trade in illicit wildlife products is transnational. According to UNODC's definition, wildlife and forest crimes are those related to any possession, consumption, trade, import, or export of fauna and flora in violation of national or international laws. The supply of many such products is concentrated in a few countries, such as rhinoceros in Africa; and demand comes from entirely different countries, such as rhino horns for traditional medicine in Vietnam. According to UNODC (2016b), the supply of such products is concentrated in Sub-Saharan Africa and Southeast Asia, and most demand comes from China and other East Asian countries, the United States, and Europe. Buyers seek illicit wildlife products for, for example, commercial products, uses in traditional medicine, or exotic pets (Dalberg 2012; Haken 2011). The Convention on International Trade in Endangered Species of Wild Fauna and Flora (CITES), the main treaty to protect endangered plants and animals, entered into force in 1975; 182 states are currently parties. Given the central role of wildlife and forestry for the ecosystem and given the fragility of endangered species, the Sustainable Development Goals also set specific targets to combat poaching and trafficking of protected species.

Since the early 2000s, transnational wildlife trafficking has been heading up. Despite the unavailability of time series data on global seizures,

Figure 1.12   Domestic poaching incidents and transnational seizures

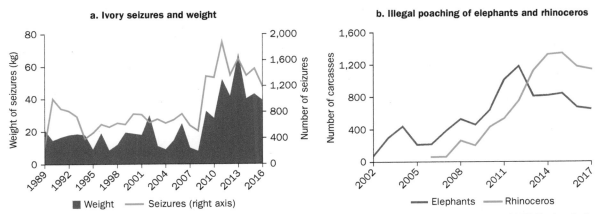

Sources: Emslie, Milliken, and Talukdar 2016; Convention on International Trade in Endangered Species of Wild Fauna and Flora (CITES) Elephant Trade Information System (ETIS) dataset, https://cites.org/eng/prog/etis/index.php, and Monitoring the Illegal Killing of Elephants (MIKE) dataset, https://cites.org/eng/prog/mike/; Save the Rhino Poaching Statistics, https://www.savetherhino.org/rhino-info/poaching-stats/.

trends for specific species indicate that illicit trade is on the rise. Data on the scale of illicit wildlife trade are based on proxy indicators, such as detected carcasses or seizures by customs authorities.[15] For example, seizures of illicitly traded ivory have drastically increased since 2008 in terms of both number of seizures and weight of total seizures (figure 1.12, panel a). Despite some decline in 2011, the level of seizures remains considerably higher than those observed over the period 1990–2008. Statistics on poaching show similar upward trends after 2005, and some decline after 2011, but remain considerably higher than in the previous decade (figure 1.12, panel b). The international trade of legal mammoth ivory, which can be a proxy for total elephant ivory demand, has also constantly increased since the late 1990s. Regarding rhinoceros, poaching has also surged from fewer than 100 per year to more than 1,000 since 2013 before leveling off (figure 1.12, panel b).

Populations of key protected species are estimated to be declining because of poaching. Since the 1960s, the population of black rhinos has shrunk from 100,000 to 5,000 (UNODC 2016b). Since 2002, the population of Indian tigers has shrunk by an estimated 50 percent (Haken 2011) and that of African elephants by 62 percent; the geographical habitat of the latter has shrunk by 30 percent (Maisels et al. 2013). On the basis of birth and natural mortality rates estimated by Wittemyer et al. (2014), elephant populations started to decline after 2010. Although estimates of the magnitude of illegal wildlife trade are highly uncertain, the annual value of illicit wildlife trafficking excluding fisheries and timber has been estimated at US$7.8 billion to US$10 billion (Haken 2011). Much of this traffic flows across borders, but the estimates include the value of both domestic and transnational trafficking. Unregulated fisheries generate an estimated US$4.2 billion to US$9.5 billion and illicit timber trade an estimated US$7 billion (Dalberg 2012).

Maritime piracy

Maritime piracy is classified as a transnational crime, because it often takes place when vessels are in international waters. Even attacks that take place within the territorial waters of a country are classified as transnational because vessels and their crews often originate from other countries. Piracy usually involves either stealing cargo or hijacking vessels and kidnapping crew to be held for ransom.

Since 2005, global levels of non-Somali piracy have steadily averaged 200–250 attacks a year. In 2018, 201 attacks were reported, of which 149 were successful and 52 were attempts (IMB 2019). Much of the data on the global scale of maritime piracy comes from the International Maritime Bureau (IMB) Piracy Reporting Centre, but underreporting can cause gaps in the data.[16] The numbers of attacks were much higher from 1999 to 2005 (figure 1.13).

Figure 1.13 Piracy attacks, 1991–2018

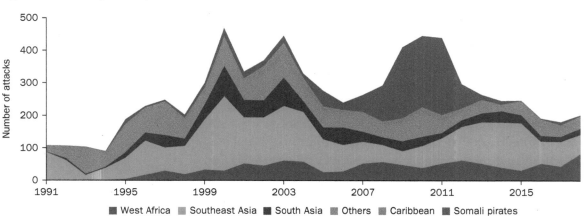

Source: IMB 2019.

Most piracy is isolated within a few regions. Most notable among these is the region between Indonesia, Malaysia, and the Philippines. The narrow straits of Malacca, Makassar, Singapore, and Sunda constitute important shipping routes; and the fact that these straits contain thousands of islets and outlets for rivers makes them ideal for pirates to attack vessels and evade capture. Another region of increasing importance is West Africa, where in 2018 there were 82 attacks, more than any other area. Of these attacks, 79 were in the Gulf of Guinea (IMB 2019).

The rise and fall of Somali piracy offer insights into what drives this transnational crime. Between 2005 and 2012, Somali pirates were responsible for over 981 attempted and 217 realized hijackings of ships in the Arabian and Red Seas and the Gulf of Aden; 198 vessels and their crews were hijacked, and the total ransom paid out is estimated at US$339 million to US$413 million (World Bank 2013). UNODC (2011a) estimated that nearly 1,400 individuals in two networks were involved in piracy along the Somali coast. Somali pirates were also distinguished from pirates in other regions because they did not rely on narrow straits that made it difficult for naval vessels to escape attacks but pursued targets into open oceans. Besley, Fetzer, and Mueller (2015) estimated that, in 2008 alone, shipping vessels whose paths exposed them to Somali pirates had to incur an additional US$630 million in shipping costs due to taking longer routes.

A World Bank (2013, 10) study conducted jointly with the UNODC and Interpol found that the primary motivations of these pirates were pecuniary. The income generated was "reinvested into the financing of future pirate operations and … support[ed] the purchase of real estate, investment in the khat trade, and other business investments and ventures." The study also found that many of those who participated "had never truly experienced safety or security, and the political and economic situation in Somalia provided little opportunity for people to find sustainable employment" (World Bank 2013, 11). Since 2012, however, Somali pirate attacks have been almost completely eliminated, mainly because of "the combined efforts of navies in the region, along with the hardening of vessels, employment of privately contracted armed security teams and the stabilizing factors of the central government within Somalia" (IMB 2013, 24).

Small arms trafficking

Very little is known about the scale of global arms trafficking. Although flows of most illicit commodities are continuous, the trafficking of firearms is episodic—partly because, unlike narcotics or animal products, firearms are durable and partly because modern weaponry is considered mature technology and has not been much improved in the past 50 years (UNODC 2011a). Further, much of this trade reportedly takes place "on a small scale and involves unsophisticated methods, such as a few handguns being transported over a border concealed in the back of a car" (UNODC 2015, 2). As a result, no reliable information is available on the extent of the illicit market for small arms and ammunition. Despite the lack of information, UNODC (2011a) estimates put the size of the illicit arms market at 10–15 percent of global legal arms trade, which as of 2017 amounted to US$1.3 billion to US$2.0 billion. Although a second source of information is customs office seizures of illicit arms, these depend on the ability of law enforcement agencies to effectively intercede in arms trafficking routes, which differs by country and agency and over time. In 2017 only 25 countries reported seizures to the World Customs Organization's Customs Enforcement Network (CEN) database (WCO 2018, 7).

Conclusion

This first chapter documents the extent to which conflict, crime, and violence have become internationalized in recent years. It details several dimensions of the internationalization in many different domains: intrastate conflicts increasingly involve nations and fighters from outside the conflicted country; the number of transnational terrorist attacks has quintupled in the past decade; the flows of refugees fleeing violence are distributed widely across receiving countries; global exports of opium, cocaine, and other illicit drugs are at a 30-year high; and piracy in international waters remains a significant threat. All these trends reflect the extent to which failures of political stability and law enforcement in one country now have dramatic effects not only on neighboring countries but also beyond. The chapter postulates that these trends are mostly driven by the dramatic reductions in the costs of trade, travel, and communication in recent decades, although data constraints make it difficult to document this association empirically. The transborder spillovers of conflict, crime, and violence are expected to gradually intensify and expand geographically as the world becomes increasingly integrated and as climate change and other global trends affect economic livelihoods and heighten the pressure on social and political stability.

ANNEX 1A The geographic dispersion of refugees

Data

The data on refugees come from the UNHCR, which since 1851 has annually published data on refugees pairing source and destination countries. The UNHCR Population Statistics Database contains data for 1951–2017 (released on June 19, 2018). The UNHCR compiles information provided by the authorities of each receiving country. The data consist of stocks of refugees and asylum seekers annually by source (223 countries) and destination (197 countries). For this analysis, refugee flows were calculated by taking the difference between two consecutive years. Although in principle the data are recorded starting in 1951, for the first few decades coverage is far from complete. The analysis therefore concentrates on the last 30 years, 1987–2017, a period for which coverage is fairly adequate. Overall, there were about 53,000 flows over the period.

Stylized facts

More recent refugees travel farther and to more destinations. Figure 1A.1 plots the five-year moving average of the distance traveled by a refugee over time. Although the time pattern is nonmonotonic, and in the past decade or so the refugee flows mostly went to closer countries, much of the period shows a gradual upward trend in the average distance a refugee traveled. From the early 1990s to 2006, the average distance a refugee traveled went from less than 2,000 kilometers to nearly 3,000 before declining. Figure 1A.2 plots the five-year moving average of the share of worldwide refugees going to an adjacent country. Starting in the early 1990s, about 85 percent of refugees fled across the border to an adjacent country. In the mid-2000s that share fell to just over 50 percent before heading up slightly in the past decade. Even with the increase in the latest five-year period, the 70 percent going directly across a border was considerably less than in 1990.

Finally, the analysis assesses whether the changes in the distance traveled and the share going to an adjacent country are driven by the changes in the pattern of source countries over time. For instance, if conflicts that stimulated refugee flows occurred in more-remote countries over time, then distance traveled would increase—not because it is now easier for refugees to travel farther but because of the change in the geography of conflict.

Figure 1A.1 Average distance traveled by a refugee, five-year moving average, 1991–2017

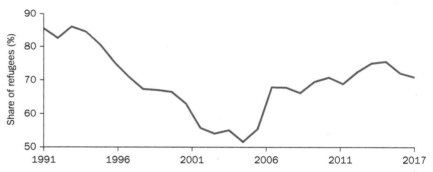

Source: United Nations High Commissioner for Refugees Population Statistics Database, http://popstats .unhcr.org/en/overview.

Figure 1A.2 Share of refugees going to a contiguous country, five-year moving average, 1991–2017

Source: United Nations High Commissioner for Refugees Population Statistics Database, http://popstats .unhcr.org/en/overview.

To rule out pure compositional changes, the analysis estimates the following regression for the source-time period:

$$Movement_{st} = \delta_t + \delta_s + \varepsilon_{st}, \qquad (1A.1)$$

where $Movement_{st}$ is either log average distance traveled by a refugee or share of refugees going to a contiguous country, from country s in time period t, and δ_t and δ_s are time and source-country effects. In particular, the source country effects imply that the analysis exploits time variation within a source country in how far refugees travel. The coefficients of interest are the time effects, δ_t. The regression estimate is weighted by total refugee outflow to obtain estimates of how outcome variables changed at a refugee rather than a country level. Standard errors are clustered at the source country. Figure 1.5 in the main text plots the time effects for the average distance traveled with 95 percent confidence intervals. Because the distance traveled is in logs, the coefficients can be interpreted as the percentage increase in the average distance traveled by a refugee in period t relative to the omitted period, which in this case is the first five years of data. The average distance traveled has clearly increased, conditional on source country fixed effects. Relative to the first period, the coefficients become significant: later in the sample, average distance traveled is as much as 60 percent higher than in the base period. The figure also shows a reversal during the period that was hit by the 2008 financial crisis.

Figure 1.6 in the main text plots the time effects for the share of refugees going to a contiguous country. Here, because the outcome variable is a share, the coefficients should be interpreted as an absolute change in the share (that is, −0.1 would mean that the share fell, for example, from 80 percent to 70 percent). Once again, conditional on the country fixed effect, the smaller share going to a contiguous country is apparent. The coefficient estimates are large, with the share going to a contiguous country falling by as much as 30 percentage points relative to the beginning.

Another manifestation of the increasing geographical reach of refugees is the greater number of their destination countries. To document a more diversified set of destinations over time, the Herfindahl index of refugee shares is computed by destination for each source country in each time period and the average across countries taken for that time period. That is, for a specific source country s and time period t, the Herfindahl index is found by

$$H_{st} = \sum_d \left(\frac{flow_{sdt}}{\sum_{d'} flow_{sd't}} \right)^2, \qquad (1A.2)$$

where $flow_{sdt}$ is the number of refugees from s to d at time t. The simple mean of H_{st} is reported for each year and then its five-year moving average is plotted. The Herfindahl index takes a maximum value of 1 when all refugees from s go to the same d, so that destination's share is 1. The lower the Herfindahl index, the more scattered the destinations of refugee flows.

Figure 1.7 in the main text plots the five-year moving average Herfindahl. The clear downward trend implies greater diversification of the destinations of refugee flows over time. Because the Herfindahl is a simple average by source country at a given point in time, it may be dominated by smaller source countries that do not account for many refugees. To check whether this is driving the results, the analysis tested the evolution of the average Herfindahl for only the top-10 and top-5 source countries in each year (which countries are so classified changes from year to year because conflict occurs in different countries). The pattern of increased source diversification is quite similar for the top source country sample.

It may be that more distance traveled over time and the falling share of refugees going to contiguous countries are simply artifacts of refugee diffusion. That is, following an impulse created by a conflict event, refugees go to the nearest country and then move farther afield, so that both the distance traveled and the share of refugees in contiguous countries fall mechanically. Figures 1A.1 and 1A.2 do not suggest that this slow diffusion is the dominant feature of the data-generating process—the trends in average distance traveled and the share going to contiguous countries are quite nonmonotonic. Unfortunately, the data do not allow for direct evaluation of the empirical relevance of this effect because they report how many refugees are present in a destination country at a point in time, not when those refugees left their home country. It is possible, however, to assess how important the slow diffusion is using several exercises detailed in the background paper (Devictor et al. 2019). In sum, the analysis does not find that the results reported here are driven mechanically by diffusion over time.

Together, the two findings imply that wealthy countries are now more affected than they had been by refugee inflows. That is indeed the case. Figure 1A.3 (panel a) plots the share of worldwide refugees that go to the wealthy OECD countries, and figure 1A.3 (panel b) plots the share that go to Europe. In the early 1990s, just 10 percent of refugees ended up in a high-income OECD country. By the mid-2000s, before falling somewhat, the share had grown to nearly 35 percent. In the most recent period, the share is above 20 percent, still double the value in the early 1990s. The pattern for refugees coming to Europe is even more pronounced. Despite some fluctuations, mostly driven by the 2008 financial crisis that hit the Euro area and OECD countries particularly strongly, at the beginning of the 1990s only about 10 percent ended up in Europe. In the most recent data, the share is 40 percent.

Figure 1A.3 Refugees fleeing to wealthy OECD and European countries, five-year moving average

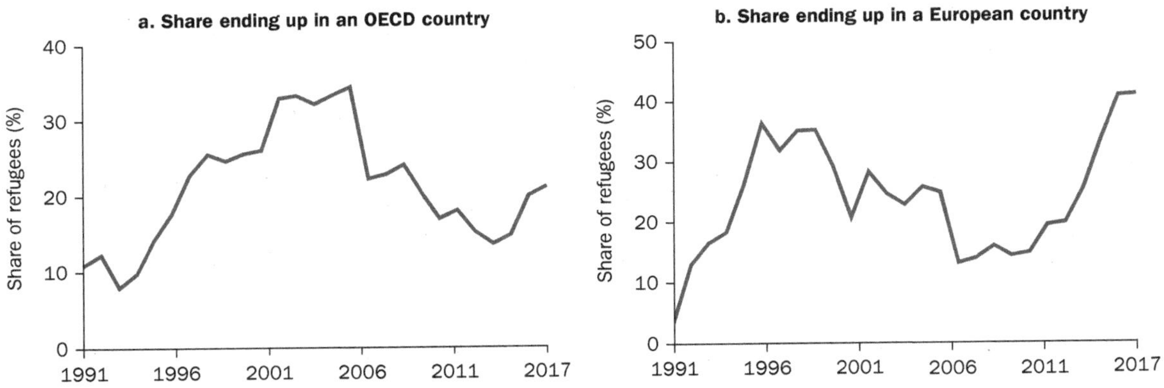

a. Share ending up in an OECD country

b. Share ending up in a European country

Source: United Nations High Commissioner for Refugees Population Statistics Database, http://popstats.unhcr.org/en/overview.

Note: OECD = Organisation for Economic Co-operation and Development.

Notes

1. Statistics from the UCDP/PRIO Armed Conflict Dataset, version 19.1, https://www.prio.org/Data/Armed-Conflict/UCDP-PRIO/.
2. The estimates of the costs of armed conflict are based on five factors, each with its own unit of measurement. Costs associated with fatalities—from terrorism as well as from both internal and external armed conflicts—are based on adjusted unit costs from McCollister, French, and Fang (2010). GDP loss estimates are based on Collier's (1999) estimates of 2.2 percent for each year of active conflict. Costs associated with displacement are based on UNHCR (United Nations High Commissioner for Refugees) annual spending and the production and consumption losses resulting from people who were part of the labor market. Costs associated with the import of small arms are sourced from the Small Arms Survey. These estimates are presented with the caveat of data quality and methodological limitations. Specifically, these estimates are prone to potential upward bias due to double counting because the estimates include costs associated with fatalities (based on an imputation of the economic value of each life-year lost) as well as GDP losses per year of conflict (from Collier 1999). Recent work by the World Bank (2017) finds that the welfare losses associated with the misery of survivors can potentially be larger than the one associated with the loss due to decreasing life expectancy. Moreover, Organski and Kugler (1977, 1980), Przeworski et al. (2000), and Miguel and Roland (2011) all document postwar economic recovery whereby countries return to their prewar growth trends after some 20-year reconstruction period.
3. Data from UNHCR's Population Statistics Database, http://popstats.unhcr.org/en/overview.
4. A Herfindahl index is a continuous measure of how concentrated the flow of refugees is. An index of 0 indicates that every country hosts the same number

of refugees; the Herfindahl index takes value 1 when all refugees go to one single country.

5. The G-7, or Group of Seven countries, consists of Canada, France, Germany, Italy, Japan, the United Kingdom, and the United States.

6. The world is projected to warm by 2–4 standard deviations by 2050.

7. The shortage of studies of the long-run effects of climate change makes it difficult to find exogenous variations that can be interpreted as causal. These may be larger than short-term effects if the effects compound over time. It is also possible that the long-run effects could be smaller if people, policies, and institutions adapt to the changing environment.

8. From the Global Terrorism Database. For more information, see http://www.start-dev.umd.edu/gtd/using-gtd/.

9. From the GTD's information on data collection methodology, https://www.start.umd.edu/gtd/faq-2/.

10. For a further review of the discussion on the overlap between terrorism and armed conflicts, see Findley and Young (2012) and Laitin and Shapiro (2008). Stanton (2013) provides a discussion for the variation in the use of terrorism as a strategy within civil wars, and Bueno de Mesquita (2013) models the rebel incentives for utilizing different kinds of violence within their activities.

11. For more information on the BAAD dataset, see https://www.start.umd.edu/baad/database.

12. The analysis identified every group responsible for more than 10 attacks since 2000 and manually identified country of origin for each. This allowed for the expansion of coverage to over 90,000 individual attacks, most of which took place after 2000 (about 46 percent of all attacks). Restricting the sample to attacks that resulted in at least one fatality, almost 52 percent of all post-2000 attacks can be attributed to the countries of origin of the groups responsible.

13. These figures are based on reclassifying ISIS attacks outside of Iraq as transnational even if these were claimed by local ISIS affiliates because of the global nature and agenda of the group. Although this reclassification may raise concerns for overestimating transnational attacks, recoding all those attacks that take place by ISIS affiliates within the countries where they are based as subnational does not substantially alter the trend; 11 percent of all attacks in 2017 still remain transnational in nature.

14. Although the UNODC compiles statistics on the number of cases and detected victims of human trafficking across 97 countries, the ILO (2017) provides estimates of bonded laborers and victims of sexual exploitation (domestic and transnational) through nationally representative surveys in 48 countries. Whereas the UNODC (2018b) estimates the total number of detected victims of human trafficking for 2016 to be about 25,000 and the US Department of State (2018) estimates 68,000, the ILO (2017) suggests that about 5.7 million people globally suffer from transnational human trafficking (3.5 million victims of forced sexual exploitation and 2.2 million victims of bonded and forced labor).

15. Reliable data on illicit wildlife trade are scarce, with countries self-reporting statistics based on cues such as carcasses or detections of illegal trade. Many countries fail to report data on seizures of illicit wildlife trade to the UNODC

which operates the global World Wildlife Seizures (World WISE) database. More robust statistics are available for only a few species, from, for example, the Elephant Trade Information System (ETIS), which collects data on ivory seizures. A common proxy for illegal wildlife poaching is carcass statistics. For instance, Monitoring the Illegal Killing of Elephants (MIKE) has been collecting elephant carcass data from conservation area rangers in 60 sites across 30 countries since 2002, providing not only the number of carcasses but also the cause of death.

16. The IMB collects information on maritime incidents across the globe, recording numerous attributes for each incident, such as location, date, boat, crew size, crew member nationalities, boat type, tonnage, and flag as well as the circumstances of the incident.

References

Alamir, A., C. Bozzoli, T. Brück, and O. J. De Groot. 2018. "The Global Economic Burden of Violent Conflict." ECARES Working Papers 2018-35, Université Libre de Bruxelles, Brussels.

Anderton, C. H., and J. R. Carter. 2011. "Conflict Datasets: A Primer for Academics, Policymakers, and Practitioners." *Defence and Peace Economics* 22 (1): 21–42.

Ansorg, N., F. Haas, and J. Strasheim. 2013. "Institutions for Sustainable Peace: From Research Gaps to New Frontiers." *Global Governance* 19 (1): 19–26.

Asal, V., and A. M. Hoffman. 2016. "Media Effects: Do Terrorist Organizations Launch Foreign Attacks in Response to Levels of Press Freedom or Press Attention?" *Conflict Management and Peace Science* 33 (4): 381–99.

Baum, M. A., and Y. M. Zhukov. 2015. "Filtering Revolution: Reporting Bias in International Newspaper Coverage of the Libyan Civil War." *Journal of Peace Research* 52 (3): 384–400.

Bayer, R., and M. Rupert. 2004. "Effects of Civil Wars on International Trade, 1950–92." *Journal of Peace Research* 41 (6): 699–713.

Besley, T., T. Fetzer, and H. Mueller. 2015. "The Welfare Cost of Lawlessness: Evidence from Somali Piracy." *Journal of the European Economic Association* 13: 203–39.

Bocquier, P., and H. Maupeu. 2005. "Analysing Low Intensity Conflict in Africa Using Press Reports." *European Journal of Population* 21 (2/3): 321–45.

Bueno de Mesquita, E. 2013. "Rebel Tactics." *Journal of Political Economy* 121 (2): 323–57.

Burke, M., E. Miguel, S. Satyanath, J. A. Dykema, and D. B. Lobell. 2009. "Warming Increases the Risk of Civil War in Africa." *Proceedings of the National Academy of Sciences* 106 (49): 20670–74.

Calderón, L., O. R. Ferreira, and D. A. Shirk. 2018. "Drug Violence in Mexico: Data and Analysis through 2017." Justice in Mexico, Department of Political Science and International Relations, University of San Diego.

Carpenter, D., T. Fuller, and L. Roberts. 2013. "WikiLeaks and Iraq Body Count: The Sum of Parts May Not Add Up to the Whole—A Comparison of Two Tallies of Iraqi Civilian Deaths." *Prehospital and Disaster Medicine* 28 (3): 223–29.

Collier, P. 1999. "On the Economic Consequences of Civil War." *Oxford Economic Papers* 51 (1): 168–83.

Dalberg (Dalberg Global Development Advisors). 2012. *Fighting Illicit Wildlife Trafficking: A Consultation with Governments.* Gland: World Wildlife Fund International.

De Groot, O. J. 2010. "The Spillover Effects of Conflict on Economic Growth in Neighbouring Countries in Africa." *Defence and Peace Economics* 21 (2): 149–64.

Dell, M., B. F. Jones, and B. A. Olken. 2014. "What Do We Learn from the Weather? The New Climate-Economy Literature." *Journal of Economic Literature* 52 (3): 740–93.

Devictor, X., Q.-T. Do, C. Le, and A. A. Levchenko. 2019. "The Geographical Dispersion of Refugees." Background paper for this report, World Bank, Washington, DC.

Donnay, K., E. T. Dunford, E. C. McGrath, D. Backer, and D. E. Cunningham. 2018. "Integrating Conflict Event Data." *Journal of Conflict Resolution* 63 (5): 1337–64.

Draca, M., S. Machin, and R. Witt. 2011. "Panic on the Streets of London: Police, Crime, and the July 2005 Terror Attacks." *American Economic Review* 101 (5): 2157–81.

Drakos, K., and A. Gofas. 2006. "The Devil You Know but Are Afraid to Face: Underreporting Bias and Its Distorting Effects on the Study of Terrorism." *Journal of Conflict Resolution* 50 (5): 714–35.

Eck, K. 2012. "In Data We Trust? A Comparison of UCDP GED and ACLED Conflict Events Datasets." *Cooperation and Conflict* 47 (1): 124–41.

Emslie, R. H., T. Milliken, and B. Talukdar. 2016. "African and Asian Rhinoceroses: Status, Conservation and Trade." CoP16, Doc. 54-2-Annexe 2, CITES Secretariat, Geneva.

Ferris, E., and K. Kirişci. 2016. *The Consequences of Chaos: Syria's Humanitarian Crisis and the Failure to Protect.* Washington, DC: Brookings Institution Press.

Findley, M. G., and J. K. Young. 2012. "Terrorism and Civil War: A Spatial and Temporal Approach to a Conceptual Problem." *Perspectives on Politics* 10 (2): 285–305.

Fortna, V. P. 2015. "Do Terrorists Win? Rebels' Use of Terrorism and Civil War Outcomes." *International Organization* 69 (3): 519–56.

Gleditsch, N. P., P. Wallensteen, M. Eriksson, M. Sollenberg, and H. Strand. 2002. "Armed Conflict 1946–2001: A New Dataset." *Journal of Peace Research* 39 (5): 615–37.

Glick, R., and A. Taylor. 2010. "Collateral Damage: Trade Disruption and the Economic Impact of War." *Review of Economics and Statistics* 92 (1): 102–27.

Haken, J. 2011. *Transnational Crime in the Developing World.* Washington, DC: Global Financial Integrity.

Harari, M., and E. La Ferrara. 2018. "Conflict, Climate and Cells: A Disaggregated Analysis." *Review of Economics and Statistics* 100 (4): 594–608.

Hsiang, S. M., M. Burke, and E. Miguel. 2013. "Quantifying the Influence of Climate on Human Conflict." *Science* 341 (6151): 1235367.

IEP (Institute for Economics and Peace). 2018. *The Economic Value of Peace 2018: Measuring the Global Economic Impact of Violence and Conflict.* Sydney: IEP.

ILO (International Labour Organization). 2017. *Global Estimates of Modern Slavery: Forced Labour and Forced Marriage.* Geneva: ILO.

IMB (International Maritime Bureau). 2013. "Piracy and Armed Robbery against Ships: Annual Report." International Chamber of Commerce: Commercial Crime Services. ICC IMB, London.

———. 2019. "Piracy and Armed Robbery against Ships: Annual Report." International Chamber of Commerce: Commercial Crime Services. ICC IMB, London.

Kalyvas, S. N. 2004. "The Urban Bias in Research on Civil Wars." *Security Studies* 13 (3): 160–90.

Laitin, D., and J. N. Shapiro. 2008. "The Political, Economic, and Organizational Sources of Terrorism." In *Terrorism, Economic Development, and Political Openness*, edited by P. Keefer and N. Loayza, 209–32. Cambridge: Cambridge, UK: University Press.

Mahmoud, T. O., and C. Trebesch. 2010. "The Economics of Human Trafficking and Labour Migration: Micro-Evidence from Eastern Europe." *Journal of Comparative Economics* 38 (2): 173–88.

Maisels, F., S. Strindberg, S. Blake, G. Wittemyer, J. Hart, E. A. Williamson, R. Aba'a, G. Abitsi, R. D. Ambahe, F. Amsini, P. C. Bakabana, T. C. Hicks, R. E. Bayogo, M. Bechem, R. L. Beyers, A. N. Bezangoye, P. Boundja, N. Bout, M. E. Akou, L. B. Bene, B. Fosso, E. Greengrass, F. Grossmann, C. Ikamba-Nkulu, O. Ilambu, B. I. Inogwabini, F. Iyenguet, F. Kiminou, M. Kokangoye, D. Kujirakwinja, S. Latour, I. Liengola, Q. Mackaya, J. Madidi, B. Madzoke, C. Makoumbou, G. A. Malanda, R. Malonga, O. Mbani, V. A. Mbendzo, E. Ambassa, A. Ekinde, Y. Mihindou, B. J. Morgan, P. Motsaba, G. Moukala, A. Mounguengui, B. S. Mowawa, C. Ndzai, S. Nixon, P. Nkumu, F. Nzolani, L. Pintea, A. Plumptre, H. Rainey, B. B. de Semboli, A. Serckx, E. Stokes, A. Turkalo, H. Vanleeuwe, A. Vosper, and Y. Warren. 2013. "Devastating Decline of Forest Elephants in Central Africa." *PLoS One* 8 (3): 1–13.

Martin, P., T. Mayer, and M. Thoenig. 2008a. "Civil Wars and International Trade." *Journal of the European Economic Association* 6 (2/3): 541–50.

———. 2008b. "Make Trade Not War?" *Review of Economic Studies* 75 (3): 865–900.

McCollister, K. E., M. T. French, and H. Fang. 2010. "The Cost of Crime to Society: New Crime-Specific Estimates for Policy and Program Evaluation." *Drug and Alcohol Dependence* 8 (1–2): 98–109.

Miguel, E., and G. Roland. 2011. "The Long-Run Impact of Bombing Vietnam." *Journal of Development Economics* 96 (1): 1–25.

Miguel, E., S. Satyanath, and E. Sergenti. 2004. "Economic Shocks and Civil Conflict: An Instrumental Variables Approach." *Journal of Political Economy* 112 (4): 725–53.

Miron, J. A., and J. Zwiebel. 1995. "The Economic Case against Drug Prohibition." *Journal of Economic Perspectives* 9 (4): 175–92.

Murdoch, J. C., and T. Sandler. 2002. "Economic Growth, Civil Wars, and Spatial Spillovers." *Journal of Conflict Resolution* 46 (1): 91–110.

———. 2004. "Civil Wars and Economic Growth: Spatial Dispersion." *American Journal of Political Science* 48 (1): 138–51.

OHCHR (Office of the United Nations High Commissioner for Human Rights). 2000a. *Protocol to Prevent, Suppress and Punish Trafficking in Persons Especially Women and Children, Supplementing the United Nations Convention against Transnational Organized Crime*. Geneva: OHCHR.

———. 2000b. *Protocol against the Smuggling of Migrants by Land, Sea and Air, Supplementing the United Nations Convention against Transnational Organized Crime*. Geneva: OHCHR.

Organski, A. F. K., and J. Kugler. 1977. "The Costs of Major Wars: The Phoenix Factor." *American Political Science Review* 71 (4): 1347–66.

———. 1980. *The War Ledger*. Chicago: University of Chicago Press.

Polo, S. M., and K. S. Gleditsch. 2016. "Twisting Arms and Sending Messages: Terrorist Tactics in Civil War." *Journal of Peace Research* 53 (6): 815–29.

Przeworski, A., M. E. Alvarez, J. A. Cheibub, and F. Limongi. 2000. *Democracy and Development: Political Institutions and Well-Being in the World, 1950–1990*. Cambridge, UK: Cambridge University Press.

Rød, E. G., and N. B. Weidmann. 2015. "Empowering Activists or Autocrats? The Internet in Authoritarian Regimes." *Journal of Peace Research* 52 (3): 338–51.

Rohner, D., and B. S. Frey. 2007. "Blood and Ink! The Common-Interest-Game between Terrorists and the Media." *Public Choice* 133 (1–2): 129–45.

Rüttinger, L., D. Smith, G. Stang, D. Tänzler, and J. Vivekananda. 2015. "A New Climate for Peace: Taking Action on Climate and Fragility Risks." An independent report commissioned by G-7 members. Adelphi, International Alert, Woodrow Wilson International Center for Scholars, and European Union Institute for Security Studies, Berlin.

Sambanis, N. 2004. "What Is Civil War? Conceptual and Empirical Complexities of an Operational Definition." *Journal of Conflict Resolution* 48 (6): 814–58.

Singer, J. D., and M. Small. 1982. "Resort to Arms: International and Civil War, 1816–1980." Beverly Hills, CA: Sage.

Stanton, J. A. 2013. "Terrorism in the Context of Civil War." *Journal of Politics* 75 (4): 1009–22.

UNODC (United Nations Office on Drugs and Crime). 2011a. *The Globalization of Crime: A Transnational Organized Crime Threat Assessment*. Vienna: UNODC.

———. 2011b. *The Global Afghan Opium Trade: A Threat Assessment*. Vienna: UNODC.

———. 2015. *Study on Firearms: A Study on the Transnational Nature of and Routes and Modus Operandi Used in Trafficking in Firearms*. Vienna: UNODC.

———. 2016a. *Global Report on Trafficking in Persons*. Vienna: UNODC.

————. 2016b. *World Wildlife Crime Report: Trafficking in Protected Species*. Vienna: UNODC.

————. 2017. *The Drug Problem and Organized Crime, Illicit Financial Flows, Corruption and Terrorism*. Part 5 of *The World Drug Report 2017*. Vienna: UNODC.

————. 2018a. *Analysis of Drug Markets: Opiates, Cocaine, Cannabis, Synthetic Drugs*. Part 3 of *The World Drug Report 2018*. Vienna: UNODC.

————. 2018b. *Global Report on Trafficking in Persons*. Vienna: UNODC.

————. 2019. *Illicit Crop Monitoring Report*. Vienna: UNODC.

US Department of State. 2018. *Trafficking in Persons Report*. Washington, DC: US Department of State.

van Ballegooij, W., and P. Bakowski. 2018. *The Fight against Terrorism: Cost of Non-Europe in the Fight against Terrorism*. Brussels: European Parliamentary Research Service.

WCO (World Customs Organization). 2018. *Illicit Trade Report*. Brussels: WCO.

Weidmann, N. B. 2015. "On the Accuracy of Media-Based Conflict Event Data." *Journal of Conflict Resolution* 59 (6): 1129–49.

————. 2016. "A Closer Look at Reporting Bias in Conflict Event Data." *American Journal of Political Science* 60 (1): 206–18.

Wittemyer, G., J. M. Northrup, J. Blanc, I. Douglas-Hamilton, P. Omondi, and K. P. Burnham. 2014. "Illegal Killing for Ivory Drives Global Decline in African Elephants." *Proceedings of the National Academy of Sciences* 111 (36): 13117–21.

World Bank. 2010. *Innocent Bystanders: Developing Countries and the War on Drugs*. Washington, DC: World Bank.

————. 2011. *World Development Report 2011: Conflict, Security, and Development*. Washington, DC: World Bank.

————. 2013. *Pirate Trails: Tracking the Illicit Financial Flows from Pirate Activities Off the Horn of Africa*. Washington, DC: World Bank.

————. 2017. *The Toll of War: The Economic and Social Consequences of the Conflict in Syria*. Washington, DC: World Bank.

————. 2018. *Asylum Seekers in the European Union: Building Evidence to Inform Policy Making*. Washington, DC: World Bank.

Zhukov, Y. M., and M. A. Baum. 2016. "How Selective Reporting Shapes Inferences about Conflict." Working paper.

CHAPTER 2

Transborder Determinants of Crime, Conflict, and Violence

This chapter documents how events beyond the boundaries of a country can influence conflict and crime within its borders. To do so, the chapter presents the results of a review of studies on conflict, crime, and violence from the fields of economics, criminology, and political science. Guiding the review of the literature, both theoretical and empirical, is a proposed unified framework that is general enough to address phenomena like drug trafficking, terrorism, and insurgency.

The analysis in this chapter begins with a simple theory based on a standard contest success function formulation. In the model two opposing agents decide how much effort to devote to violence, according to the expected costs and benefits of such investments. In doing so, each party takes into account the decisions of the other party. This theory identifies four risk factors related to conflict, crime, and violence: the opportunity cost of participation (how well participants would fare in alternative activities), the value of the "prize" (the gains to the winner), state capacity, and the intrinsic (nonmonetary) benefits of participation. The chapter then reviews the evidence on factors external to a country that affect the occurrence of domestic conflict, crime, and violence. The theory is used to structure the literature review, recognizing the difficulties of constructing clear empirical proxies for the model's theoretical parameters.

After reviewing the empirical literature on transnational determinants of conflict, crime, and violence, the chapter zeroes in on two instruments a foreign country or coalition of countries can use to purposefully alter the violence trends of another country—military interventions and development assistance. The review makes it clear that how these interventions affect violence is ambiguous and highly context-specific. The evidence also allows for revisiting the security–development nexus. The chapter concludes by discussing the theoretical rationales for third-party interventions to promote peaceful solutions, by reducing problems related to information asymmetries or limited commitment.

The theoretical framework

The theoretical framework models insurgency, organized crime, or terrorism as activities that combine inputs like labor (for example, soldiers, gunmen, suicide-bombers) and capital (for example, weapons, vehicles, information acquisition) in the pursuit of a prize that may be ideological, political, or financial. For instance, the objective of rebel groups that wage civil war is usually control over certain territory rather than production of an illegal good or service. Some forms of crime require criminal syndicates to control swaths of territory for either extortion (as in the case of a mafia) or production and transportation of illicit products (for example, drugs). One can view these activities as a means of contesting the state's monopoly on the use of force. Thus, the review follows scholars of political science and economics and models the outcome of rebellions and some forms of criminal activities as a *probability* of seizing control over a disputed territory. Terrorism and other criminal activities like human or wildlife product trafficking, however, are a means of escaping law enforcement. In the model used for this chapter, the outcome would translate into the probability of successfully eluding apprehension by law enforcement authorities.[1]

This probability of success is modeled in a contest game framework. A contest game models the probabilities of each party's winning as dependent on the investments made by that party and by everyone else. Because such contest success functions are well suited for examining the strategic interactions between warring parties,[2] such games have become workhorses in the study of conflict (Esteban and Ray 2011; Garfinkel 1990; Garfinkel and Skaperdas 2007; Skaperdas 1992, 1996). To clarify the main insights offered by the model and to guide the discussion throughout this report, this chapter presents a simple version of a contest game. A formal exposition of the model is given in annex 2A.

The forms of violence discussed in this report are viewed as the outcome of a strategic interaction between two parties—with one labeled the government G and the other a contestant T. T can be viewed as an insurgent group, a terrorist organization, or a criminal syndicate. Both parties fight over a prize valued at A.[3] Each party makes a security investment, M_G for the government and M_T for the contestant. The investment comes at a unit cost of c_G to the government and c_T to the contestant. When dealing with conflict, the investment is military and can consist of either labor (for example, hiring soldiers or insurgents) or capital (for example, buying weapons). For crime or terrorism, government investments can be seen as the deployment of law enforcement assets. The probability that the government will win the contest is given by a function $P(M_G, M_T)$, where the probability is increasing in the government's investment M_G, and is decreasing in the contestant's investment M_T. The probability that the contestant will win is therefore $1 - P(M_G, M_T)$. For instance, a popular functional form is to make the probability of winning proportional to the share of government investment in total investment:[4]

$$P(M_G, M_T) = M_G / (M_G + M_T). \qquad (2.1)$$

What drives the investment decisions of contestants? Each contestant takes the opponent's action as given and chooses its own investment so as to maximize its payoff. In other words, a contestant takes M_G as given and chooses M_T to maximize its net payoff, which is the expected value of the prize (the probability of success multiplied by A) minus the total costs incurred to make investment M_T or $c_T M_T$. Similarly, the government takes M_T as given and chooses M_G to maximize its net payoff, considering unit cost c_G for doing so. In other words, each player responds "optimally" to the other player's choices.

The intersection of these two optimal-response curves indicates the Nash equilibrium of the contest game, with the security investments of the two parties (see figure 2.1). The horizontal axis measures government security investments; the vertical axis captures the investments of the contestant. The blue line plots the investment response of the contestant to any given level of security investment from the government. Symmetrically, the orange line represents the government's best response to the contestant's own security investments. The dotted 45-degree line is characterized by equal investments by both opponents, hence there is an equal probability of success—50 percent—for both parties.

The figure shows the government with a relatively lower cost of making military investments than the contestant, hence the higher equilibrium security investment by the government and, consequently, a higher probability of government success (see annex 2A for the technical details, including the exact cost functions used to generate the figure). Because contest games do not directly map these strategic investments into violence levels, the probability of success of the contestant is posited as a measure

Figure 2.1   Equilibrium in a contest game

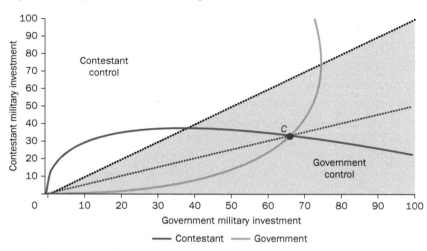

Source: Original figure for this report.

Note: C = equilibrium point.

of conflict violence or crime incidence (see annex 2A for more detailed discussion). Thus, any point on a line going through the origin is character-ized by the same level of violence: as the line rotates clockwise, violence dampens; when it rotates counterclockwise, violence heightens.

Diving deeper into the cost function of the contest model allows for generation of empirically testable predictions about the drivers of conflict. In particular, the model assumes that one party needs to recruit personnel to engage in the crime or conflict-related activity, such as fighters to join a rebellion, suicide bombers to carry out a terror attack, or gunmen to par-ticipate in an illegal business. For an individual, the decision to become the contestant is viewed as an occupational choice problem (annex 2A discusses the individual's decision problem). Participants choose between a legitimate sector that pays a wage w and a violence sector that remunerates partici-pants either with a monetary reward r in case of success or a punishment s in case of failure; the punishment could be a fine, a prison sentence, injury, or death. It is also possible that individuals derive an intrinsic, nonmone-tary, benefit b from participation in conflict, such as utility from doing one's patriotic duty or helping to redress an old grievance against the oppos-ing party. The recruiting party thus needs to compensate participants for the opportunity cost of their time (the alternative wage w) but also for the risk they take. Either party to the conflict may also choose to emphasize the intrinsic benefits, via propaganda or threats, which may help to lower the monetary reward it needs to pay.[5] If the probability that the contestant wins is P, then the net total reward for conflict participation is $b + P\,r - (1 - P)\,s$, which consists of the intrinsic benefit b and the payment r for success, which occurs with probability P, net of sanction s, in case of failure, which occurs with probability $1 - P$. Conflict will be chosen if the reward is greater than the opportunity cost, that is, when

$$b + P\,r - (1 - P)\,s > w. \qquad (2.2)$$

This formulation, consisting of the contest success function approach coupled with the individual's participation constraint, generates several pathways through which external influences can influence internal conflict, crime, and violence (figure 2.2).

The opportunity cost channel. The contest model predicts that, when the returns to alternative occupations w for would-be participants increase, the contestant will find it harder to recruit people to engage in crime or conflict. In figure 2.2 (panel a) an increase in the opportunity cost of violence translates into an inward shift of the contestant's reaction curve, lowering the violence. When, for example, global food prices go down, so do farmer wages, which lowers the opportunity cost of their moving to an alternative occupation. Generally speaking, when the "price" of conflict and crime inputs is lower, the opportunity cost view implies that violence will be higher. For instance, cessation of conflict in a country can lead to an inflow of fighters and weapons into a neighboring country, in effect lowering the price of both labor and capital as inputs into conflict or crime. The spread of technology might also matter, not necessarily because it lowers prices directly but because it makes it cheaper to mobilize labor and capital inputs by reducing the transaction costs associated with coordination and information dissemination.

The returns to violence or the "predation" channel. If the value A of winning the conflict is higher, both government and contestant will move more resources from productive to conflictual activities (Garfinkel and Skaperdas 2007; Grossman 1999). Unlike the opportunity cost view, the predation view emphasizes economic returns to violence as a driver of violence. An increase in the demand for illegal goods (for example, illegal drugs, wildlife products, and so on) in consuming countries will make engaging in drug trafficking or wildlife poaching more profitable in producing countries. Conversely, by providing a close substitute of the illegal good or service, market legalization can potentially reduce the returns to crime and hence its incidence.[6] If both parties value the prize equally, however, an increase in the returns to violence A shifts both response curves out, so both

Figure 2.2   Determinants of violence in the contest success function model

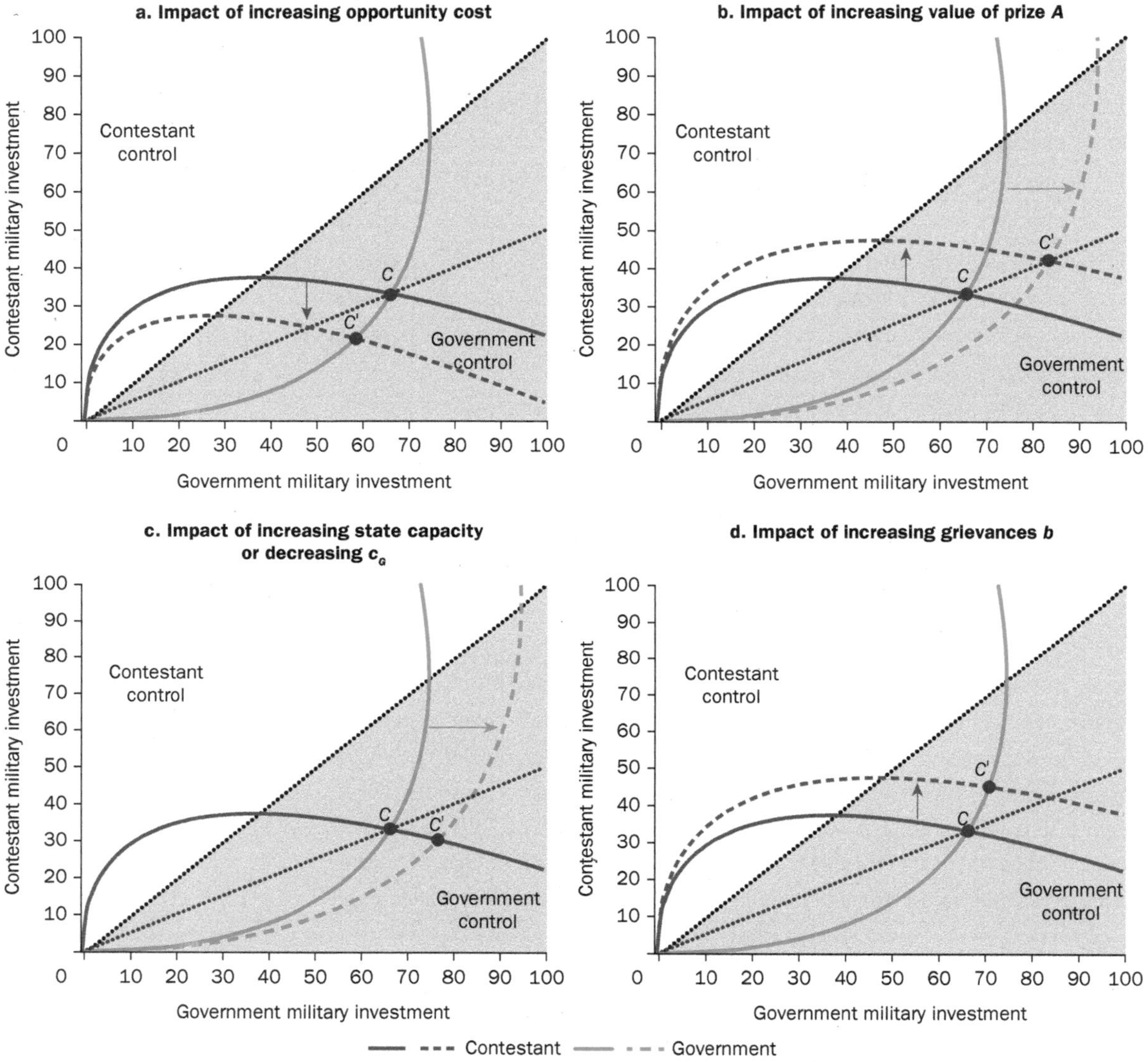

a. Impact of increasing opportunity cost

b. Impact of increasing value of prize _A_

c. Impact of increasing state capacity or decreasing _c_G

d. Impact of increasing grievances _b_

- - - Contestant   - - - Government

Source: Original figures for this report.

Note: **Panel a:** _C_ is the original equilibrium: in the new equilibrium _C'_, both government and contestant invest less in military resources, and overall level of conflict decreases. **Panel b:** _C_ is the original equilibrium: in the new equilibrium _C'_, both government and contestant invest more in military resources, but overall level of conflict stays the same. **Panel c:** _C_ is the original equilibrium: in the new equilibrium _C'_, government invests more and contestant invests less in military resources, leading to a reduction in conflict. **Panel d:** _C_ is the original equilibrium: in the new equilibrium _C'_, both government and contestant invest more in military resources, and conflict increases.

parties increase their security investments (Fearon 2008). The effect on conflict violence, therefore, is ambiguous: higher contestant investments are met with more government deterrence: depending on which curve shifts out farther (see figure 2.2, panel b), violence may be lessened, be worsened, or remain unchanged. As an illustration, although spikes in mineral prices may make the prospects of an insurgency more attractive by increasing the returns from seizing territory and capturing the revenues from natural resources, they equally increase government incentives to maintain control, making the net effects on violence theoretically ambiguous.

The "state capacity" channel. An increase in state capacity would entail a decrease in the government's cost c_G of undertaking security investment M_G. The cost captures the ability of the government to deploy military to fight insurgencies or law enforcement to fight crime, but it also affects the government's fiscal constraints. Figure 2.2 (panel c) illustrates an increase in state capacity, which leads the government's response curve to shift outward, decreasing violence. The same forces that affect the opportunity cost of participating in conflict and crime might also influence the state's capacity to build and deploy military or law enforcement assets to deter conflict, crime, and violence. They may not only affect the cost of these assets, as is the case for criminal organizations and insurgent groups, but also change the state's fiscal space. Thus, large changes in the terms of trade, such as changes in oil prices, can positively affect the capacity of oil-exporting countries and negatively affect the capacity of oil-importing ones.

The "grievance" channel. When the intrinsic benefits from conflict or crime participation b increase—say because the individual has a grievance against the government or for ethnic, religious, or political reasons is aligned with an insurgent organization—it becomes easier for the contestant to recruit individuals. Thus, a larger grievance and a smaller opportunity cost have the same effect in that they shift the response curve of the contestant outward (figure 2.2, panel d). The level of conflict therefore rises. The nonmonetary benefits of participation could be positive, when there is social prestige from joining a rebel group or a criminal enterprise, or negative, when there is a social stigma for doing so. Thus, to the extent that economic shocks abroad affect economic growth and government revenues, they might impinge on the government's ability to provide adequate public services, such as social safety nets, and so exacerbate societal grievances. Alternatively, cross-border flows of information and ideas might also affect citizens' expectations of their governments and potentially become a source of discontent.

Transborder drivers of conflict, crime, and violence

The literature on the determinants of both conflict and crime have been mainly concerned with within-country determinants of violence (see, for example, Blattman and Miguel 2010 for a review of civil wars and Draca and Machin 2015 for a review of economic incentives and crime). One of the most robust results of these studies is the fact that low-income countries are more likely to experience conflict, whereas the estimated relationships with other hypothesized variables, such as economic inequality or ethnic diversity, are inconclusive. Global market integration, by contrast, subjects a country to outside influences. Although that finding is interesting for this report in its own right, global factors also serve as an exogenous source of variation in socioeconomic conditions that is beyond the direct control of domestic agents. Thus, many studies based on global shocks are able to overcome the methodological barriers to establishing causal relationships.

Events in one country can affect the socio-politico-economic equilibrium in another through multiple channels. Global market integration means that goods and services move across borders. Such mobility has price implications because domestic returns to specific activities are now subject to international forces. In addition to goods and services, technology, information, and ideas also flow across borders. Previous research has noted that global market integration can have implications for both the amount of income and its distribution.[7]

International shocks to demand and supply

When countries are integrated into world markets, goods and services that are traded are subject to world prices. An exporting country can thus be affected by either demand or supply shocks beyond its borders through several pathways. An increase in the price of a commodity raises the price of the factors of production (capital or labor) of that commodity, raising the opportunity cost of participation in violence. Higher commodity prices can also mean higher revenues from exploiting that commodity. These increased rents can generate more fiscal revenues for the government that increase state capacity or heighten the incentives to commit crime or join a rebellion because the returns to violence are now higher. Which channel will operate or dominate thus depends on both the commodity affected and how the proceeds from its sale are distributed. It is therefore not surprising that the initial studies of the relationship between commodity prices and conflict often had contradictory results.[8]

Recent studies on commodity prices have carefully considered how different commodities can change different determinants of conflict. Specifically, higher prices for agricultural commodities, which tend to be more labor-intensive, are likely to raise the opportunity cost of engaging in conflict and thereby to reduce conflict (see figure 2.2, panel a). When Dube and Vargas (2013) examined the impact of global coffee prices on insurgent activities in Colombia, they found that municipalities where a large proportion of land area is devoted to the crop are more likely to be affected by world coffee price fluctuations. Consistent with the opportunity cost channel, they found that for such municipalities a fall in coffee prices resulted in a large and statistically significant increase in conflict intensity. They estimated that, during the international coffee crisis of 1997–2003, the 68 percent fall in coffee prices was responsible for "an additional 1,013 war-related deaths in Colombia's coffee cultivation areas" (Dube and Vargas 2013, 1403). They also found very similar results for the impact of prices of sugar, bananas, palms, and tobacco. Part of the increased casualties can be explained by the fact that lower coffee prices enable insurgents to switch from irregular, hit-and-run attacks to more conventional frontal assaults (Wright 2016).

The relationship between agricultural prices and conflict in Colombia generalizes to a larger sample of countries and commodities. Using disaggregated data on conflict events for subnational units of 0.5 × 0.5 degrees latitude and longitude, and matching them to local suitability for 45 different crops and using variations in total world demand for them, Berman and Couttenier (2015) found that higher demand for a region's agricultural commodities reduces the incidence of conflict in that region. McGuirk and Burke (2018) similarly found that rising food prices significantly reduce the onset and duration of conflict in food-producing areas and increase the probability of conflict in consuming areas.[9]

When prices surge for commodities that require little labor input, or in areas that can be easily captured by violent tactics, the returns to violence are likely to go up. Dube and Vargas (2013) examined the impact in Colombia of a change in the price of a nonagricultural commodity, oil. In stark contrast to their findings that higher prices for coffee lowered conflict, they found that an increase in world oil prices results in a significant increase in paramilitary attacks in oil-rich municipalities. They attributed the difference to the fact that higher coffee prices typically increase work hours and wages, which supports the opportunity cost view, but uptakes in oil prices do not increase wages but rather increase municipal revenues.

The jump in paramilitary attacks is therefore probably driven by the higher benefits to violence, in this case the capture of oil-rich municipalities. Berman et al. (2017) reached a similar result, using disaggregated data on 14 minerals for African countries (for subnational units of 0.5 × 0.5 degrees latitude and longitude). They found that a spike in mineral prices increased conflict risk in cells producing those commodities; the rise in commodity prices over 1997–2010 explains 14–24 percent of the concurrent rise in violence in African countries. Although this cross-country study finds that mineral price spikes fuel both low-level violence (riots, protests) and organized violence (battles), this outcome is not necessarily the case in every country (see Christensen 2019 for an analysis of South Africa). Similarly, McGuirk and Burke (2018) found that higher food prices increased the probability of reports by commercial food producers of thefts and violence. In contrast, Axbard, Poulsen, and Tolonen (2016) found that a US$10 rise in international mineral prices led to an increase in the number of active mines in South Africa and reduced violent crimes by 6.6 percent and property crimes by 8.8 percent. Symmetrically, the closing of mines caused a spike in crime rates. Clearly, when mineral price increases translate into increases in employment, the opportunity cost channel is in play.

Empirical evidence related to the state capacity channel is as yet relatively scarce. The existing literature on the impact of larger government revenues points to ambiguous effects, because such revenue-based increases in state capacity might also lead to higher incentives to capture rents. Asher and Novosad (2019) detected a significant increase in the presence of criminal politicians in India when world mineral prices rise, together with an increased propensity to commit crimes and accumulate rents. As documented by Sexton (2019) in the case of Peruvian municipalities during mining booms, however, corruption might be controlled when politicians are held accountable by either high administrative capacity or strong political competition (World Bank 2016). Finally, Armand et al. (2019) found evidence of both the conflict-increasing and the conflict-mitigating channels using data from Mozambique. They first documented that, on the one hand, receiving information about future resource rents can increase elite capture and rent-seeking behavior by local leaders (that is, a deterioration in state capacity), even when the resource rents in question have not yet materialized. On the other hand, information and deliberation targeted at citizens increase mobilization and accountability and decrease violence.

The transborder spillovers of domestic regulation and policies

Regulatory or policy changes in one country can affect the propensity for civil conflict, crime, and violence in neighboring countries and beyond. These policies, sometimes described as "beggar-thy-neighbor" policies, change product prices, especially when the country is a large player, as either consumer or producer, on the market. Reductions in the value of an illicit product can be expected to lower violence, by lowering the returns to conflictual activity (see figure 2.2, panel b). In the context of transnational illegal markets, policies in importing countries have, through changes in prices, an impact on exporting countries; similarly, policy changes in exporting countries can affect violence in importing countries. For example, Dube, Dube, and García-Ponce (2013) documented the impact of a change in US gun laws on violence in Mexican municipalities bordering the United States; they posited that the expiration of a 2004 federal ban on assault weapons in effect lowered the price of such weapons by increasing the supply. They found that gun seizures increased following the regulatory change—and so did violent crime. Similarly, Knight (2013) found that guns used in violent crimes are transported from states with weak gun laws to states with strong ones, and that cross-state spillovers mostly occur between contiguous states.

Spillover effects have also been observed in the illicit wildlife trade. Do et al. (2018) estimated the price elasticity of elephant poaching in Africa. By establishing that prices in a major consumer market pass through to prices in Africa at a unit rate, they estimated the impact of Chinese market regulation on poaching in African countries and found that a 10 percent reduction in black market ivory prices would reduce elephant poaching by 4.4 percent. Consequently, the two-thirds drop in ivory prices in 2017 attributed to China's recent decision to close its domestic market for ivory (Vigne and Martin 2017) would reduce poaching of African elephants by one-third.

Regulations not directly related to price, such as legalization of formerly illegal goods and services, constitute an alternative mechanism by which crime and violence in one country can be affected by policies adopted by other countries. For instance, drug legalization can be expected to lower the prices of formerly illicit drugs and thereby reduce the returns to violence in the drug market. Though relatively few estimates of illicit goods prices exist, they suggest that such price differentials can be large: Miron (2003) estimated that black market prices were 3 times higher than legal prices for heroin, and 19 times higher for cocaine. As expected, drug legalization by some US states has been shown to reduce crime rates in other states, particularly those that border Mexico (Gavrilova, Kamada, and

Zoutman 2017). Furthermore, in the illegal trade for drugs, such changes affect not only producer countries but also transit countries or regions because a higher price for drugs would increase the returns to all actors along the supply chain—smugglers as well as producers. Higher prices thus lead to increased predation for control of production and smuggling networks, with an associated rise in violence (Dills, Miron, and Summers 2010; Fajnzylber, Lederman, and Loayza 2002a, 2002b; Soares 2006).

In the study of human trafficking, however, the lack of data and variations in regulation make it difficult to get information on transborder spillovers. For the United States, Cunningham and Shah (2018) found that decriminalizing indoor prostitution not only led to a drop in prices due to increased supply, locally and across state borders, but also lowered the incidence of rape and the prevalence of sexually transmitted infections.

As with spillovers of regulation on illicit commodities, spatial displacement may arise in response to a crime reduction program. The displacement of crime as an undesirable outcome for targeted policing has been an important theme in the criminology literature for some time (Reppetto 1976). Many of these studies focus on the impact of high-crime hot-spot policing using an experimental or quasi-experimental evaluation of policing interventions (Braga et al. 1999; Sherman and Rogan 1995; Weisburd and Green 1995). A subsection of these studies on targeted police interventions also focused on the "diffusion" of crime into control areas. Many of these earlier studies had mixed results, ranging from a diffusion of lower criminal activity in treatment areas with higher criminal activity in control areas (Reppetto 1976) to positive spillovers of targeted policing to untargeted areas (Clarke and Weisburd 1994). Most recent studies, however, as well as those by economists do not find a strong and persistent displacement of crime (Di Tella and Schargrodsky 2004; Draca, Machin, and Witt 2011; Jacob, Lefgren, and Moretti 2004; Weisburd et al. 2006). Barr and Pease (1990) argued that displacement can take place both geographically, when criminals move to nontreatment areas, and temporally, with criminals postponing activities until the end of the treatment; criminals might also diversify into other illicit activities not being directly targeted.

Conflict contagion

Another channel through which countries can be affected by events outside their borders is conflict contagion. Contagion occurs when conflicts in one country alter the likelihood of a conflict later taking root in a different country (Forsberg 2014). This diffusion entails both tangible factors—such as flows of arms, fighters, and economic resources—and less tangible processes through which conflict in one country provides lessons, inspiration, and clues for actors in other countries or exacerbates international disputes. For both mechanisms, much of the academic inquiry on contagion has studied contiguous neighbors (Bara 2018; Beardsley 2011; Braithwaite 2010; Forsberg 2008; Gleditsch, Salehyan, and Schultz 2008; Hammarström 1994; Kathman 2010; Most and Starr 1980, 1983; Salehyan and Gleditsch 2006; Siverson and Starr 1990). Although this distinction makes intuitive sense—the mechanisms for transmission are at least partially geographic—any empirical exercise that advantages proximity in space over other transmission channels risks both under- and over-identifying instances of contagion (Black 2013). More recent papers have moved to examining factors beyond simple geographical proximity (Black 2013; Buhaug and Gleditsch 2008; Fox 2004; Kathman 2011; Maves and Braithwaite 2013).

The main methodological hurdle for researchers is to distinguish contagion from interdependence. Establishing a causal link requires ruling out alternative mechanisms that would also predict a correlation between conflict in one country and a higher likelihood of conflict in neighboring countries. In particular, as noted earlier, one proximate cause of conflict is economic shocks, which can be correlated between trading partners. Most studies account for this by assuming that interdependence can be accounted for by controlling for such variables as observed gross domestic product or trade flows (Murdoch and Sandler 2002, 2004). Another methodological difficulty is correctly specifying the time lag by which contagion takes place. Some scholars suggest that these are immediate externalities that take time to taper off (Beardsley 2011; Black 2013; Kathman 2011); researchers have typically adjusted by including lags between one and five years into their neighborhood conflict coding. Bara (2018, 1993) argued, however, that, "within the first year of post-conflict peace, the probability of spillover more than doubles." Her argument is that the cessation of hostilities in one location, which results in both unemployed rebels and unused military equipment, can provide an avenue for contagion into a neighboring country, where they bolster the war-making abilities of domestic groups. She finds that the probability of conflict outbreak for an average country increases by 71 percent if the country neighbors a country that witnesses a cessation of conflict in the last three years, even controlling for other active conflicts within neighboring countries.

Technology diffusion

Technology diffusion across borders can affect the incidence of crime, conflict, and violence because it lowers the cost of mobilizing financial resources, recruiting personnel, and coordinating actions of criminals or militants on the ground. Beyond logistics, technology can also be used to spread ideas that will ultimately alter how the population perceives the government—the grievance channel. Alternatively, technology can enhance state capacity by giving government a more effective means of communication, propaganda, or deterrence.

Many studies have documented the importance of communication technologies in mobilizing resources in conflicts. Yanagizawa-Drott (2014) found that radio broadcasts in Rwanda that encouraged violence against the Tutsi minority population had a significant impact, explaining about 10 percent of the participation in killings by both militia groups and ordinary civilians. Similarly, Della Vigna et al. (2014) showed how exposure to a Serbian nationalist radio station incited anti-Serbian sentiments in Croatia; Manacorda and Tesei (2016) found that the diffusion of mobile phones in Africa explains part of the increased protest turnout observed between 1998 and 2012; and analysis by Enikolopov, Makarin, and Petrova (2018) showed that protest activity in the Russian Federation during the 2011 "Snow Revolution" was enhanced by the use of social media.

The same communication technologies can also be used to reduce conflict or change the nature of societal grievances. Armand, Atwell, and Gomes (2017) documented how radio messaging encouraged defections from the Lord's Resistance Army rebel group operating in the Central African Republic, the Democratic Republic of Congo, South Sudan, and Uganda and thus reduced conflict events and fatalities. In a similar vein, Shapiro and Weidmann (2015) found that the expansion of the cell phone network in Iraq over 2004–09 reduced insurgent violence, possibly because of a greater ability for noncombatants to provide information. In a yearlong experiment, Paluck (2009) examined subjects who were exposed to a reconciliation soap opera on Rwandan radio that featured messages about reducing intergroup prejudice, violence, and trauma. Compared to the control group, those in the experiment group were significantly more favorable to intermarriage and showed signs of enhanced trust, empathy, and cooperation. Blouin and Mukand (2019) similarly found that exposure to the government-controlled Radio Rwanda, which promoted messages emphasizing Rwandan identity rather than ethnic cleavages, made ethnic identities less salient and increased interethnic trust.

Overall, the evidence base suggests that countries are increasingly subject to the effects of events and policies from outside their borders over which they have little control. Nevertheless, national governments and multilateral agencies can work to reduce individual or country exposure to dramatic changes in commodity prices. Sovereign wealth funds are a typical example of instruments that can help smooth government budgets over time. National governments can also use instruments like social safety nets to shelter citizens from real income shocks due to external factors. Given the potential for transborder spillovers from political instability, the international community also has incentives to act as insurer of last resort. Market regulation of some tradable goods and services also has transborder implications. Global market integration thus implies the need for increased policy coordination across countries.

Can violence be avoided?

Why rational actors may engage in violence

The previous analysis has considered factors that could increase or decrease the intensity of conflict. A natural question that arises is why all parties engage in violence that imposes social and economic costs on both sides rather than agreeing to a peace deal that would give them the same returns while avoiding the costs of violence. In terms of the model, if the government would win with probability P, it should be willing to accept a share P of the overall "prize," which would leave it with the same expected returns but without incurring the cost of violence. Although military investments might be made to improve the bargaining position, parties should still be willing to accept a division of the resources without resorting to violence. In the case of crime, wherever there are societal externalities from criminal activity, the same rationale applies: because there is a surplus from avoiding violence that could be shared between the participating parties, a negotiated settlement that avoids the social costs is likely to be feasible. Figure 2.3 shows the "cone of feasible peace agreements" in the context of the model: any division of resources within that cone is strictly preferable to one involving security investments and conflict; each party would accept a smaller share if it is from a bigger pie. Annex 2A formally derives the boundaries of the cone of possible resource allocations.

In these circumstances, it is natural to ask why both parties cannot reach an agreement to share resources before security investments are made or actual confrontation occurs.

Figure 2.3 **Contest game and the cone of possible resource allocations**

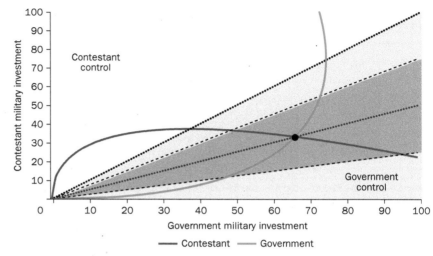

Source: Original figure for this report.

Note: The orange line shows the reaction function of the government to the contestant's military investment, whereas the blue line shows the contestant's reaction function (as in figures 2.1 and 2.2). The area shaded blue demarcates the range of military investments where both sides would be willing to accept a peaceful agreement rather than resorting to violence. Note that this area includes the original conflict equilibrium, the point where the two reaction curves intersect.

The necessary conditions for a peaceful resource allocation to be accepted by both parties are the following: (1) agents are rational; (2) they understand both their own costs and benefits and those of their opponent (in particular, they know the probability of winning); and (3) all parties are able to commit to a previously agreed course of action (perfect commitment). These arguments were first formulated by Fearon (1995), who refers to the failures of conditions (2) or (3) as "rationalist explanations for war." Fearon was reflecting on a large body of academic research in political science, international relations, and economics that attempted to explain failures to reach peaceful agreements that would avoid conflict and violence in the first place. The main arguments are summarized here; more detailed discussions can be found in Garfinkel and Skaperdas (2012).

Information asymmetries: Violence as signaling

The simplest formulation of the information asymmetry argument is that both parties overestimate their probability of winning and therefore do not agree to the peaceful settlement. In principle, of course, they could share information about their own costs and benefits with the other party to facilitate peaceful negotiation. Because both parties would have incentives to misrepresent their strengths ("cheap talk"), however, states might have to undertake costly actions to communicate their real strength. In such situations, according to Fearon (1995, 397), "a rational state may choose to run a real risk of (inefficient) war in order to signal that it will fight if not given a good deal in bargaining." A large body of literature has provided formal underpinnings for this logic and identified implications that match the data observed. Models that incorporate asymmetric information match the prediction that wars are more likely to happen in poor countries (Dal Bó and Powell 2009), and even a small amount of information asymmetry can be enough to generate arms races and conflict outbreaks (Baliga and Sjöström 2004; Chassang and Padró i Miquel 2010).

Issues of information asymmetry often worsen with the involvement of multiple parties. Esteban and Ray (2001) showed that, with four or more agents involved in a negotiation, and even a minimal lack of information, a Pareto-improving social decision rule becomes impossible— that is, there is likely to be conflict over the division of resources. These arguments are consistent with empirical evidence that civil wars tend to be significantly longer when they involve more factions that can act as veto players (Cunningham 2006).

A different motivation for violence is to intimidate or signal intentions to a third group, namely community members. Criminal gangs may threaten violence to prevent community members from sharing information with the police; a similar logic applies to insurgent groups that need support from the general population to be viable. Here again, the exercise of violence is viewed as a credible signal from insurgents or criminals of their willingness and ability to retaliate. In other words, as emphasized by Kalyvas (2006), violence in civil wars may be not just an outcome variable but also a process variable. Both theoretical and empirical analyses of detailed microdata on insurgent groups have shown that, like the governments they oppose, insurgents often use targeted violence to coerce civilian populations into giving them support—or at least withholding support from the enemy (Azam and Hoeffler 2002; Chenoweth and Lawrence 2010; Kalyvas 2006; Kalyvas and Kocher 2009; Wood 2010). A related motivation for criminal gangs may be to build a reputation for violence to deter resistance from their victims and thereby extort more from them (Leeson 2009).

Limited commitment

A reason often cited for why peace deals are difficult to reach and sustain is a lack of commitment by one or all parties (Powell 2006). The limited commitment argument is distinct from information asymmetries in the sense that all participants have full knowledge of each other's costs, benefits, and probability of success. They may not be able to avoid violence today, however, if they (correctly) anticipate that tomorrow the calculations may change. For example, Fearon (2004) laid out a case where a government can face exogenous shocks to its capabilities (for example, an economic crisis or a significant reduction in aid funds) that change its strength relative to a rebel group. During periods when a government is relatively weak, it has an incentive to provide higher payoffs to the rebel group in order to secure peace. But the government also has an incentive to renege on the deal when it is relatively strong. If the government cannot commit to not renege on its pledge, insurgents will not agree to a peace deal in the first place.[10]

Commitment problems are more likely to arise when actors on either side do not have a long-term horizon. For instance, when agreements signed by one government can be revoked by the next government that comes to office, commitment may be incomplete. This view is consistent with empirical evidence that documents increased drug-related violence in Mexican municipalities that were more electorally competitive (Dube, Dube, and García-Ponce 2013; Osorio 2015). Besley and Persson (2011) argued that peace is more likely when institutional capacity (for example, democratic institutions) exists to make long-term commitments and limit diversion of resources. This can be one explanation for the observed phenomenon of "democratic peace"—that is, democratic countries rarely go to war against other democratic countries.

The presence of multiple actors can worsen the commitment problem. For instance, it can be difficult to negotiate peaceful settlements in a setting with many different criminal or terrorist organizations because no single criminal syndicate or terrorist or insurgent group can represent all current and future criminal syndicates or terrorist or insurgent groups.

A special case of "multiple actors" arises when the leader who makes decisions about violence and peace has a different cost–benefit calculation than the group as a whole. For instance, some leaders may bear a disproportionate share of the costs from a war, whereas others may be able to capture a disproportionate share of the gains. The formal model of Jackson and Morelli (2007) demonstrated that even with complete information violence may still occur in the presence of such "political bias." If both parties are unbiased, however, at most only one party will choose to forgo a peaceful settlement. Assuming that democracies are more likely to be unbiased, that is, that the costs and benefits as understood by the leader are more closely aligned to those of the whole population, this model provides an explanation for the observed phenomenon of democratic peace.

Foreign military interventions and development assistance

Among the external influences a country is exposed to, two types of foreign involvement are specifically intended to alter domestic policies or the socio-politico-economic landscape: development aid and military interventions. The effect of either on violence is conceptually ambiguous, because these interventions can affect multiple parameters of our theoretical framework. Not surprisingly, the empirical evidence on their impact also shows mixed and context-specific results. Recent studies have shed some light on how multiple channels operate, but more research on these topics is needed to help guide policy makers.

Trends over recent decades have shown a clear increase in both foreign aid and military interventions in civil conflict. Using Organisation for Economic Co-operation and Development (OECD) data on net official development assistance (ODA) from the OECD Development Assistance Committee (DAC) countries (which include most member countries), in the last four decades, in constant US dollars foreign aid has more than tripled, from about US$40 billion in the mid-1970s to almost US$150 billion in 2017.[11] Further, between 1989 and 2003 international actors intervened in fewer than 20 percent of civil conflicts; between 2004 and 2017 these interventions jumped to about 55 percent, spiking noticeably after the 9/11 attacks (see details in chapter 3).

Other means of influencing cross-border violence trends, such as targeted economic sanctions (including trade restrictions) or measures to restrict terrorism financing, have been less studied—partly because of insufficient data to properly identify policy details and partly because of the difficulty of constructing an effective counterfactual scenario. Box 2.1 reviews the literature related to targeted economic sanctions, and box 2.2 provides some information on countering terrorism financing.

Most of this chapter's review of the impact of aid and military intervention on conflict, crime, and violence will be structured around how these factors affect the parameters of our theoretical model. Both military interventions and aid have the potential to affect multiple parameters in the theoretical framework, so that the net effect of such interventions is

Box 2.1 Sanctions

Sanctions are foreign interventions in which one or more foreign countries impose coercive measures on a specific government or entity within a country to incite a change in policy or behavior and prevent certain undesirable outcomes (Escribà-Folch 2010). In terms of public opinion or finances, economic sanctions are seen as less costly than direct military interventions while providing an alternative way to align incentives. Countries and multilateral organizations have significantly expanded the use of economic sanctions since the end of the Cold War (Weiss 1999).

The international community imposes economic sanctions for reasons that range from protecting human rights and promoting democratic change to retaliation and coercion of a country that violated the sovereignty of another country (Neuenkirch and Neumeier 2015; Stremlau 1996; Weiss 1999). Recently, sanctions have also been used to punish states that protect terrorists. For example, since 2014, the US government has imposed economic sanctions on several countries that were declared "state sponsors of terrorism." Countries experiencing civil war are often targets of sanctions—for example, the former Yugoslavia in 1991, Cambodia in 1992–97, Rwanda in 1994–95, and Côte d'Ivoire in 1999–2002.[a] Economic sanctions may take the form of restrictions on exports and imports or on economic assistance (or of a freeze on a country's assets abroad) and have different degrees of intensity (from threats, to minor restrictions, to full embargoes). As documented by Ahn and Ludema (2019), over the last decade sanctions have shifted from broad trade embargoes to sanctions targeted to specific transactions, individuals, or companies.

The evidence base on the effectiveness of sanctions is small and mostly suggestive, for at least two reasons. First, sanctions are imposed for a variety of reasons and with different objectives, often not clearly stated, which makes it difficult to measure the outcome of interest. Second, because sanctions are country-specific, it is often difficult to determine an appropriate counterfactual for comparison, namely a country similar enough but that is not subject to sanctions. The evidence available is consistent with the view that economic sanctions are effective at destabilizing regimes and have an impact on their economies. Targeted regimes have been seen as characterized by a lower probability of survival in office for regime leaders (Marinov 2005); they experience per capita gross domestic product growth that is slower by 2 percentage points (Neuenkirch and Neumeier 2015); and they have a poverty gap 3.8 percentage points higher than countries not subject to sanctions (Allen and Lektzian 2013). Regimes may react to the resultant political instability, however, by increasing repression (Wood 2008), thus worsening human rights and triggering an increase in extrajudicial killings, torture, or political imprisonment (Peksen 2009). Ahn and Ludema (2019) analyzed sanctions against firms in the Russian Federation after the invasion of Ukraine and found that "strategic" firms selling high-priority goods to the regime systemically outperformed nonstrategic firms under sanctions, suggesting that the target government may be able to shield some firms from the full brunt of the sanctions.

The impact of economic sanctions on conflict is mixed. In theory, sanctions can also shorten wars by reducing the expected payoffs of victory or by increasing the imbalance between the opposing parties. Different forms of interventions (including sanctions) can also lengthen a civil war if they shift the balance of power between the parties toward more parity (Regan 2002) or introduce new veto players that limit the range of peace agreements (Cunningham 2006). Empirical studies reflect this ambiguity, with Escribà-Folch (2010) finding that economic sanctions are associated with shorter conflicts and Hultman and Peksen (2017) finding that economic sanctions actually increased conflict fatalities.

(continued)

Box 2.1   continued

Lektzian and Regan (2016) showed that economic sanctions reduce the duration of conflict only when accompanied by military interventions.

a. Data from the Peterson Institute for International Economics web page "Summary of Economic Sanctions Episodes, 1914–2006," https://www.piie.com/summary-economic-sanctions-episodes-1914-2006.

Box 2.2   Anti-money laundering and combatting the financing of terrorism

Although traditional notions of money laundering may relate to the concealing of sources of illegitimately obtained money, these same channels are also used for the purpose of transmitting funds to finance illicit activities. At the nexus of these two related activities lie transnational criminal markets and the financing of terrorism and insurgencies. Behind the revenue estimates for different illicit markets in chapter 1, an entire network of money laundering sustains these activities. Because of the illicit nature of these activities, however, precise figures are unavailable. A United Nations Office on Drugs and Crime study estimated that, in 2009, over US$2.1 trillion of profits generated by illicit market organizations was laundered—equivalent to 3.6 percent of global gross domestic product (UNODC 2011a). Of this amount, almost 70 percent was laundered internationally through financial markets whereas the rest either was spent domestically or was lost or appropriated within criminal organizations. On the other end, it is estimated that terrorist groups and insurgents acquire much of their financing through these same networks. Despite the unavailability of precise estimates, one example of this acquisition of financing is that nearly US$150 million was raised from the opium trade in the form of taxes on production and through extortion to finance the Afghan insurgency in 2011 (UNODC 2017)—equivalent to 38 percent of the group's total income for the year (UNODC 2011b).

As opposed to sanctions, countries can adopt voluntary reforms to adhere to international standards of anti-money laundering and combatting the financing of terrorism (AML/CFT) in order to improve their access to global financial networks. AML/CFT international standards were first established by the Financial Action Task Force (FATF) in 1990 in direct response to "misuse of financial systems by persons laundering drug money" (FATF 2019, 6). Since then, these standards have evolved and currently consist of 40 recommendations dealing with AML as well as the inclusion of 9 special recommendations aimed at combatting terrorism financing—together, the FATF 40+9. Although economic sanctions are imposed bilaterally, failure to comply with the FATF's recommendations carries no direct penalties. It may, however, result in the imposition of sanction or the restriction of a noncooperative country's access to financial markets. A 2011 International Monetary Fund study found that the average level of compliance on FATF recommendations remains low (45 percent and 31.5 percent for AML and CFT recommendations, respectively) (Verdugo Yepes 2011).

Research on the quality of AML/CFT policies is limited because of difficulties in identifying and tracking illicit transactions. UNODC (2011a) estimated that less than 1 percent of illicit financial flows were seized and successfully frozen. Further, because of limited information on the experience of law enforcement with AML/CFT activities, their relative efficacy is not well understood, leading some researchers to conclude that one-size-fits-all AML policies may instead have severe negative effects on developing country growth (Bartlett and Ballantine 2002).

theoretically ambiguous. The review of the empirical literature reflects this ambiguity, with no overall consensus on whether aid and military interventions increase or decrease conflict. More recent empirical work focused on specific parameters has found more consistent results. This section concludes with some thoughts on the "security–development nexus" or the interrelationship between military interventions and aid flows.

Foreign military interventions

Direct military interventions and military aid to increase a government's capacity to deter insurgent, criminal, or terrorist groups are often used in fragile countries. How such actions affect violence and conflict is ambiguous: On the one hand, they enhance the repressive technology of governments and law enforcement—facilitating the targeting and apprehension of insurgents, terrorists, or criminals—and enhance government deterrence and incapacitation capacity. This corresponds to an increase in state capacity, or a reduction in the government's unit cost, c_G in the model (see figure 2.2, panel c). On the other hand, additional repressive technology can worsen grievances b, in particular when there is collateral damage to civilians. The first factor would help reduce violence; the second would exacerbate it. There is increasing recognition that civilian cooperation with the government by, for example, providing information about insurgent activities and plans (Berman, Shapiro, and Felter 2011) or by adopting community norms that impose social sanctions for participation in violence (Akerlof and Yellen 1994) is likely to be an important factor in the success or failure of violent actors, because the population of recruits who participate actively in crime, terrorism, or rebellion is usually a very small fraction of the total population. Thus, in terms of the theory, the net effects of military intervention are unclear.

Similarly, empirical studies have also found mixed results for the impact of military interventions on conflict and crime. Several papers have documented a reduction in crime or conflict after foreign armed interventions. Where crime is concerned, Do, Ma, and Ruiz (2016) found that, although the deployment of international naval assets off the coast of Somalia did reduce pirate activity, a bigger factor was the presence of privately contracted armed security personnel on board the largest vessels. Studying the impact of US drone strikes in Pakistan, Mir and Moore (2018) found a significant reduction in insurgent violence attributable both to the loss of insurgent personnel and to the deterrent effects of perceived higher risk. Crucially, they found no evidence that the drone strikes resulted in greater support or recruitment by the Pakistan Taliban, which suggests that, in that context, the increased-grievances channel was not very strong. Johnston and Sarbahi (2016) similarly documented a reduction following drone strikes in the number and lethality of terrorist attacks. The results are also mixed on the impact of assassinating or capturing the leaders of terrorist groups, with some studies finding that such events do not lead to group dissolution (Jordan 2009), whereas other studies find a strong negative effect on terrorist group survival (Price 2012).

Several other studies have found that military interventions lead to greater future violence, which suggests that in some contexts the increasing grievances effect can be greater than the deterrence effect. Areas that were subject to heavier US aerial bombardment in Vietnam were more likely to end up controlled by the Viet Cong (Dell and Querubin 2018; Kocher, Pepinsky, and Kalyvas 2011). US airstrikes in Afghanistan also resulted in increased insurgent attacks (Lyall 2019). Focusing on military aid from the United States, Bapat (2011) found a positive correlation between military aid and how long terrorist groups survived. Condra and Shapiro (2012) analyzed geo-coded data on civilian casualties between 2004 and 2009 in Iraq. They found that coalition killings of civilians are associated with more insurgent violence against the government, whereas killings of civilians by insurgents lowered insurgent violence in the following periods—an indication that citizens withhold cooperation from the parties responsible for collateral damage.

A few recent studies provide more explicit measures of citizen attitudes, grievances, or willingness to cooperate. Using data from an information-sharing program in Iraq where civilians can share tips about insurgent activities, Shaver and Shapiro (forthcoming) showed that information flow goes down after government forces inadvertently kill civilians and goes up when insurgents do so. Blair, Imai, and Lyall (2014) measured citizen attitudes directly using surveys in five Pashtun-majority provinces of Afghanistan. They found strong evidence that civilian casualties inflicted by the US-led coalition in Taliban-dominated areas reduce civilian support, but that Taliban-inflicted harm does not improve attitudes toward international coalition forces.

Development assistance and conflict violence

Development assistance can affect several parameters of the model simultaneously, complicating predictions of the relationship between aid and violence. First, aid can improve livelihoods and wages, which raises the opportunity cost of participating in conflict (w). Aid can also reinforce a country's law enforcement capacity (decreasing c_G) and thus lower insurgent activity. Also, depending on how aid is spent, it can be instrumental in a country's counterinsurgency "buying-hearts-and-minds" policy and lowering grievances (b). All these factors would reduce violence. If aid funds or materials can be easily expropriated, however, more aid flows may increase the returns to violence (A).

The large empirical literature on aid effectiveness reflects this conceptual ambiguity when the impact on violence is examined.[12] Correlational studies have found no effects of total aid on conflict (Collier and Hoeffler 2002); a conflict-prolonging effect of humanitarian aid (Narang 2014, 2015); and an increase in violence perpetrated by rebel groups but not by government (Wood and Sullivan 2015). More sophisticated analyses, based on instrumental variables strategies, have also had mixed results. De Ree and Nillesen (2009) used the gross domestic product of donor countries as instruments for aid flows and estimated that a 10 percent increase in ODA reduced by 8 percentage points the likelihood that war will continue in the following period. Nunn and Qian (2014), however, used weather-induced variations in US wheat production as an exogenous determinant of food aid, and found a significant conflict-prolonging effect of greater US food aid.[13]

Studies focusing on "hearts-and-minds" initiatives have found that strategies to encourage community cooperation with the government typically have a conflict-reducing effect. In a pioneering study, Berman, Shapiro, and Felter (2011) examined a counterinsurgency program created by the US military to fund local community projects in order to enhance civilian cooperation. They found that every additional dollar of reconstruction funding in Iraq resulted in 1.59 fewer violent incidents per 100,000 population per half year. Further results suggest that the opportunity cost channel is unlikely to be the main driver: the biggest impact was observed for small rather than large grants. Similarly, Dell and Querubin (2018) compared the strategies deployed in Vietnam by the US Army, which relied on overwhelming firepower deployed through search-and-destroy raids, and the US Marine Corps, which emphasized providing security by embedding soldiers in communities and winning support through development programs. Using a regression discontinuity design, they found that hamlets just to the Marine Corps side of the boundary suffered fewer attacks by the Viet Cong, were less likely to have a Viet Cong presence, and had citizens reporting more positive attitudes toward the United States and all levels of South Vietnamese government. In India, Khanna and Zimmermann (2014, 2017) observed an increase in government-initiated violence and apprehension of insurgents after introduction of a large public works program, consistent with a mechanism of higher civilian information sharing. Similarly, conditional cash transfer programs have been shown to increase government raids against insurgents in Colombia (Weintraub 2016) and reduce rebel influence in the Philippines (Crost, Felter, and Johnston 2016). Recent work has highlighted that even small amounts of humanitarian assistance following casualties can have a large impact on subsequent violence (Lyall 2019), and that aid can lead to greater perceptions of state legitimacy even when it does not change "hearts and minds" (Böhnke and Zürcher 2013). On a cautionary note, Chou (2012) replicated the Berman, Shapiro, and Felter study (2011) for a similar reconstruction program in Afghanistan but found no significant evidence that reconstruction funding, large or small, was an effective conflict abatement strategy.

In contrast to the evidence on the efficacy of hearts-and-minds approaches, analyses that directly estimate the impact of aid on civilian attitudes are fewer and somewhat inconclusive. Examining humanitarian aid after the 2005 earthquake in Pakistan, Andrabi and Das (2017) found that receiving foreign aid led to a significant positive change in the attitudes of the local Muslim population toward Westerners that was still evident four years after the earthquake. In contrast, a community-driven development program in Afghanistan changed attitudes toward the government only in stable areas but not in insurgent-dominated ones, in spite of widespread improvements in perceived well-being (Beath, Fotini, and Enikolopov 2012).[14] Evidence is also mixed on the impact of development assistance on social cohesion. Some studies have found that community-driven reconciliation or reconstruction programs can significantly improve social cohesion (Avdeenko and Gilligan 2015 for Sudan; Cilliers, Dube, and Siddiqi 2016 for Sierra Leone; Fearon, Humphreys, and Weinstein 2009, 2015 for Liberia). One of the first randomized evaluations of a community-driven development program found no evidence of improvements in collective action, decision making, or inclusion of marginalized groups in local institutions (Casey, Glennerster, and Miguel 2012).

Postconflict programs for demobilization, disarmament, and reintegration (DDR) are typically designed to maximize the opportunity cost of returning to violence by improving the living conditions of former combatants. In one of the first evaluations of a DDR program, Humphreys and Weinstein (2008) used propensity score-matching to compare participants and nonparticipants in a United Nations–sponsored program in Sierra Leone. The results suggest that the program failed to improve economic or political integration of former combatants. More recent papers based on a natural experiment (Gilligan, Mvukiyehe, and Samii 2012 in Burundi) and randomized controlled trials (Blattman and Annan 2016 in Liberia) found much larger increases in participant incomes. The latter study found that program beneficiaries shifted work hours away from illicit activities to farm employment and expressed reduced interest in mercenary work in a nearby war.

Development assistance can also affect state capacity, but methodological constraints make it difficult to estimate a causal impact of aid on state capacity. For instance, aid is not randomly allocated to countries; Alesina and Weder (2002) found that more-corrupt countries receive more aid. In studies using instrumental variables to overcome such endogeneity concerns, some have found that aid decreases corruption (Tavares 2003) and others that higher dependence on foreign aid is associated with a worsening of democratic institutions (Djankov, Montalvo, and Reynal-Querol 2008).[15] To test the impact of aid on institutions, Rajan and Subramanian (2007) used a different strategy; they examined the relative growth of governance-intensive industries. Their findings suggest that, if aid hurts governance, the result should be a relative slowdown of industries that most depend on it, and, if it helps, those industries will accelerate. Having created an index of governance intensity based on the concentration of purchases of each industry from other sectors, they found that governance-dependent industries grow more slowly in countries that receive more aid, which suggests a negative impact of aid on institutions. A more recent analysis by Ahmed (2016) used exogenous variations in US aid coming from the degree of legislative fragmentation in the US House of Representatives and found that US aid enhances state repression and authoritarianism and weakens government accountability. These better-identified studies suggest a negative impact of aid on state capacity.

Even if the context may be suitable for a positive impact of aid on conflict or violence, a large body of evidence also indicates frequent retaliation and sabotage when an insurgent group perceives aid as a threat. For instance, insurgents in Afghanistan targeted international aid workers (close to 700 attacks in less than five years) in order to reduce the capacity of aid organizations to implement projects, and attacks were concentrated in areas with more progovernment attitudes (Narang and Stanton 2017).

Similarly, a conditional cash transfer program funded by the World Bank in Colombia led to an increase in insurgent violence against civilians (Weintraub 2016). In another widely cited paper, Crost, Felter, and Johnston (2014) used a regression discontinuity design to find that areas in the Philippines selected for a World Bank community development program experienced greater insurgent-led violence than areas not selected.

Insurgent attacks against aid initiatives are often driven by sabotage intentions, rather than by the goal of appropriating the aid money or resources. For instance, the effects documented by Crost, Felter, and Johnston (2014) were concentrated in the early stages before the World Bank program went into operation, which the authors take as suggestive evidence of the use of sabotage to prevent municipalities from successfully implementing a program. Child (2018) examined development aid and reconstruction programs in 398 districts in Afghanistan between 2005 and 2009 and found that aid projects in education led to greater conflict but that health interventions were associated with a reduction in violence. He suggested that the differential impact arises because the Taliban saw education projects as a bigger threat, given the capacity to indoctrinate. Starker evidence of strategic sabotage is provided by Condra et al. (2018), who documented that insurgent attacks in Afghanistan are two orders of magnitude higher on election days than on other days, leading to a drop of 9–14 percent in voter turnout per additional attack. It appeared that insurgents carefully chose the time and place of their attacks to minimize damage to civilians, which implies that the primary goal was to disrupt institution-building activities like elections.

Compared to the extensive literature on aid and conflict, much less evidence exists on how aid affects terrorism. Several developed countries have used aid programs as a counterterrorism instrument (Azam and Delacroix 2006). This policy has been criticized by studies that have found no robust evidence connecting poverty and terrorism. Both Krueger and Malečková (2009) and Krueger and Laitin (2008) argued that terrorists tend to come from wealthier and more educated families. The methodological challenges of establishing a causal link between aid and terror incidents are similar to those encountered in investigating how aid affects civil conflicts. Cross-country panel data studies have found that aid to a given country is associated with a reduction in terrorist attacks there (Azam and Thelen 2010a, 2010b). Young and Findley (2011) disaggregated the type of foreign aid by sector and found that the negative correlation between aid and terrorist attacks is mostly observed with education, health, civil society, or conflict prevention projects; but they found no clear association between military aid and terrorism. This finding is consistent with the theoretical mechanisms discussed earlier: the former types of aid have a greater potential to increase opportunity costs or reduce grievances or to do both, whereas military aid may increase grievances even while improving the state's ability to combat terrorism.

The literature review suggests that both theoretically and empirically the effects of aid and military interventions on conflict are ambiguous. Despite evidence to support the idea that aid can induce greater community cooperation, the results may not be generalizable to all contexts. It is worrisome, though, that aid seems to result in governance deficits and declines in state capacity. Policy makers also need to be aware that conducting aid projects in high-conflict areas can be complicated by (violent) attempts to sabotage such projects. Thus, development assistance may not satisfy the "first-do-no-harm" principle.

The security–development nexus

An important question here is the role of the "security–development nexus"— that is, the relationships between these two types of interventions. In conflict settings, moreover, aid and security interventions often influence each other because they are delivered jointly. When do aid and military interventions reinforce each other? And when do they act at cross-purposes?

Given the evidence of sabotage, it is likely that the success of aid projects often depends on the presence of military power. Extending the empirical work of Berman, Shapiro, and Felter (2011), Berman et al. (2013) found that the conflict-reducing effect of aid programs is greater for small programs and where sufficient troop presence exists to secure the area. More evidence is provided by Beath, Fotini, and Enikolopov (2012), who examined a randomized field experiment in Afghanistan where 250 municipalities were eligible for a community-driven development program in 2007 but another 250 were ineligible until 2011. They found that the program reduced violence only in areas that were already secure and had no significant impact in contested areas. A recent systematic review of 19 studies finds that aid has a violence-dampening effect on conflict zones only if a relatively secure environment exists for aid projects to be implemented (Zürcher 2017). In a randomized experiment on crime control in Bogotá, Blattman et al. (2019) found suggestive evidence for a reduction in violent crimes when both deterrence levels (police) were increased and the provision of a public good (street cleaning) was stepped up, highlighting how community cooperation can enhance the effectiveness of law enforcement.

Although the evidence base is still relatively small, it suggests that development assistance and military intervention may be complementary in some settings. Furthermore, the community can be a critical third strategic actor in the contest between government and criminals, terrorists, or insurgents: aid and military interventions both drive the attitude of the community, which in turn contributes to the effectiveness of those interventions. More research is needed, however, to better understand these relationships.

Conclusion

Crime and conflict are both activities that lower societal welfare and that increasingly affect populations outside of a country's borders. The literature on crime and civil wars has highlighted factors that mitigate the incidence of violence by either increasing the opportunity cost or lowering the net benefits of engaging in such activities. The role of the community as a critical intermediary between the state and potential criminals or insurgents has been acknowledged. A country's fiscal constraints and lack of expertise in addressing these challenges warrant assistance from foreign countries or institutions in the form of financial or technical support. Given the possibility of regional or global spillovers, the case for foreign assistance is even starker. Moreover, because events and policies adopted in one country can affect the fragility of another, the security challenges a country faces might be best addressed not with any domestic policy instrument at its disposal but with policy coordination.

The next chapter delves deeper into situations whereby a country simply does not have (or no longer has) the proper policy instruments to fight crime and prevent conflict within its borders.

ANNEX 2A   Contest model

This section formally establishes and analyzes the contest model that guided the discussion in this chapter.

A theoretical framework for the analysis of conflict, crime, and violence

The contest takes place between the government G and the contestant T. T can be viewed as an insurgent group, a terrorist organization, or a criminal syndicate. The fight is over a prize of value A. Each party makes a security investment, M_G for the government and M_T for the contestant. The investment has a unit cost of c_G for the government and c_T for the contestant. The probability that the government will win the contest is simply

$$P(M_G, M_T) = \frac{M_G}{M_G + M_T}. \qquad (2A.1)$$

In more general formulations of contest success functions, military investments are typically weighted by "investment effectiveness" parameters, which allow identical investments by the parties to have different impacts on the battlefield. For details, see Jia and Skaperdas (2012).

Contest games determine a party's best strategy for responses to its opponent.

What drives player investment decisions? Players take an opponent's action as given and choose their own investment to maximize the payoff. In other words, the contestant takes M_G as given and chooses M_T to maximize

$$\frac{M_T}{(M_T + M_G)} * A - c_T\, M_T. \qquad (2A.2)$$

The first-order condition determines the contestant's best response to a level of government security investment M_G:

$$\frac{M_G}{\left(M_T(M_G) + M_G\right)^2} * A = c_T. \qquad (2A.3)$$

The cost of an additional unit invested in security is c_T; at the optimal, it is equal to the marginal benefit, that is, the incremental increase in the payoff due to a higher probability of success.[16] The first-order condition gives the following functional form for the contestant's best response:

$$M_T(M) = \sqrt{\frac{M * A}{c_T}} - M. \qquad (2A.4)$$

Symmetrically, the government has a response to the contestant's security investments. The government's choice, which depends on its own unit cost, is determined by maximizing

$$\frac{M}{M + M_T} * A - c_G * M, \qquad (2A.5)$$

which leads to a best-response function for the government:

$$M_G(M) = \sqrt{\frac{M * A}{c_G}} - M. \qquad (2A.6)$$

Figure 2.1 shows the results of both optimizations. When both parties use their optimal response to their opponent's optimum, the system will converge to a unique outcome, which determines how much will be spent on security in equilibrium and the (stochastic) outcome of the contest.

Individual participation in conflict, crime, and violence

To take the model to the data, the analysis adds more structure to the cost function of the contestant, on the assumption that security investments for the contestant consist of hiring its labor force. To look at individual participation, the analysis considers the trade-off participants face. When individuals decide to join, they are assumed to receive some private benefit from participation, b. The private benefit measures the participant's personal or social gratification from joining the contestant; the decision to join can also be driven by political or religious alignment. When, instead, joining is associated with stigma, b is allowed to take negative values. Participants face a risky outcome: when contestants win, recruits get reward r; if they lose, sanctions s against recruits include prison, fines, injuries, or even death. If P is the probability of success for the contestant, then, assuming risk-neutrality, individuals who decide to participate get payoff $b + Pr - (1 - P)s$; however, the recruit forgoes the labor market wage w. It is assumed that the individual making a decision is taking the probability of success P as given; later, this annex discusses the possibility of multiple equilibria when P is endogenized.

Individual payoffs from participation	
Yes	No
$b + P * r - (1 - P) * s$	w

Making the assumption that the contestant sets reward r to make individuals indifferent between participation and nonparticipation pins down the contestant's cost function, that is,

$$c_T = P * r = w - b + (1 - P) * s. \qquad (2A.7)$$

The best-response function of the contestant can then be written

$$M_T(M) = \sqrt{\frac{M * (A+s)}{w-b+s}} - M. \qquad (2A.8)$$

Thus, the best-response curve of the contestant shifts up if A or b increases or w or s decreases. The government's best-response curve, conversely, shifts out if A increases or c_G decreases. Figure 2.2 illustrates these comparative statics, which are discussed in the text of the chapter.

From theory to empirics

How can these theoretical predictions be interpreted for empirical analyses? One limitation of the contest success function is that it maps security investments (defense spending, weapon purchases, soldier recruitment, and so on) into a probability of winning a contest. It does not say anything about actual violence or human or economic losses. Although the empirical literature has used the number of conflict fatalities to determine the onset of wars and their durations, no empirical endeavor appears to have clearly laid out a theory of conflict that generates testable implications in terms of casualties. Of course, because investments in security are difficult to observe (especially on the rebel side), opportunities to directly test a contest function model of conflict are rare.

One natural candidate for a measure of violence in the model could be the sum of security investments by both parties. Here, the loci characterized by equal levels of violence are concentric circles around the origin. This assumption would directly map theoretical predictions from the contest function model into measures of violence. Assuming that violence rises with the amount of security investment, however, ignores the role of deterrence. For instance, despite producing zero casualties the nuclear arms race would then be considered the most violent conflict. More generally, such an assumption would ignore the role of deterrence in reducing crime: increased law enforcement deters criminal activity and thus lowers violence. Thus, the relationship between violence and security investments ought to be nonmonotonic.

An alternative adopted in this report relies on the assumption that conflict is the most violent when the prize is most contested—that is, when the probability of winning for either party is equal to 50 percent. Then, as the probability of winning for either party decreases, so does violence. As a result, "iso-violence" curves are straight lines going through the origin.

The domain is further restricted to where the probability that the contestant will win is less than 50 percent, so that violence is minimal when the government wins with probability one (horizontal axis) and increases as the line going through the origin and the equilibrium point rotates counterclockwise. The model thus has the following properties: crime and conflict violence increase with the contestant's security investments, and crime and conflict violence decrease with the government's security investments (deterrence effect).

On the cone of possible peace agreements

Because violence destroys surplus, there is always a peaceful outcome that both contestants prefer to the division of resources under violence. In other words, each party would prefer a smaller share of a larger pie than a larger share of a smaller pie. The expected payoffs of the government in a conflict situation are given by $P\left(M_G, M_T\right) A - c_G M_G$ so that any division of the prize A so that the government gets $P_G.A$ with $P_G > P_G^* = P\left(M_G, M_T\right) - c_G \dfrac{M_G}{A}$ is preferred to the conflict game outcome. Symmetrically, a peace agreement that distributes $P_T.A$ to the contestant is strictly preferred to conflict when $P_T > P_T^* = 1 - P\left(M_G, M_T\right) - c_T \dfrac{M_T}{A}$. Thus, the two lines P_G^* and P_T^* define the cone of possible peace agreements, which is nondegenerate as $P_G^* + P_T^* < 1$.

Notes

1. Probabilistic functions have long been used to model individual decision making (Haavelmo 2015; Luce 1959). Econometricians have also used such probabilistic functions to model binary decisions (McFadden 1973).
2. The application of these functions to the theoretical study of conflict was first undertaken by Hirshleifer (1989), and they were also applied to areas as diverse as rent-seeking, firm competition, labor contract design, or sports (see Dixit 1987; Lazear and Rosen 1981; Szymanski 2003; Tullock 1980). A comprehensive analysis of contest games can be found in Konrad (2009).
3. For simplicity, the prize is assumed to have identical value for both parties.
4. Jia and Skaperdas (2012) discuss the theoretical and axiomatic foundations of the various functional forms that contest success functions can take.
5. The tension between monetary and nonmonetary rewards within an organization has received attention from scholars looking at incentives in the

workplace (see, for example, Besley and Ghatak 2005; Prendergast 2007, 2008). The present analysis abstracts from this subtlety for the time being, especially because little research has been done on this issue in the context of crime and conflict.

6. Market liberalization can, however, lead to an expansion of demand when legalization lowers the stigma attached to consumption of illicit goods like drugs, elephant ivory, or rhinoceros horns, or services like prostitution. For more detailed discussions on this issue, refer to the legal literature on the expressive function of law (see, for example, Sunstein 1996).

7. Frankel and Romer (1999) made one of the first attempts to establish a causal relationship between a country's openness to trade and its level of economic development. A large literature has also documented the distributional implications of trade (see, among others, Autor, Dorn, and Hanson 2013; Goldberg 2015; Helpman et al. 2017).

8. For instance, Brückner and Ciccone (2010) found that a 20 percent year-on-year drop in the international price of a country's main export commodities increases the probability of a civil war by 2.8 percent, whereas Bazzi and Blattman (2014) found no relationship between commodity price increases and the onset of civil war. Although some of these differences can be attributed to differences in data coverage of countries and commodities, it may also be that, in these settings, commodity prices affect the prices of both inputs into conflict and the returns to conflict, so that effects go in opposite directions. Earlier, the link between natural resources and vulnerability to conflict has been documented in cross-country associations (Collier and Hoeffler 1998, 2004; Ross 2004a, 2004b), but these associations are hard to interpret causally because of concerns about possible confounding factors.

9. Changes in domestic factor prices may be due not only to changes in international prices but also to domestic policies that increase the country's exposure to global markets. Trade policies that reduce incomes or increase unemployment tend to increase crime rates and conflict intensity. These patterns have been documented for several countries: Brazil (Dix-Carneiro, Soares, and Ulyssea 2018), India (Iyer and Topalova 2014), Mexico (Dell, Feigenberg, and Teshima 2019), and Ukraine (Zhukov 2016).

10. Finally, another reason for inability to achieve peaceful solutions relates to the "indivisibility" of the prize for which the parties are competing. For example, when the contested territory is a holy site that cannot be divided, or when law enforcement authorities seek arrest of the kingpin of a criminal or terrorist organization, indivisibility seems to imply no solution other than conflict and violence. Powell (2006), however, saw the indivisibility issue as a particular aspect of the commitment problem, because both parties could work around the indivisibility problem with a lottery. The indivisibility problem then is equivalent to the inability for the ex post loser to commit to accepting a lottery outcome. Fearon (1995) similarly argued that constraints on divisibility are likely to arise from political, social, or moral reasons to not accept the partial gains from negotiation, rather than from any inherent indivisibility of the issues themselves.

11. Data from OECD's International Development Statistics database, http://www
.oecd.org/development/financing-sustainable-development/development
-finance-data/idsonline.htm.

12. This ambiguity mirrors the inconclusive results from the large literature on
the impact of aid on aggregate income or growth (see, among many, Burnside
and Dollar 2000; Easterly 2003; Galiani et al. 2017; and a review by Qian
2015).

13. A recent reanalysis by Christian and Barrett (2017) found that the results in
Nunn and Qian (2014) may have been driven by spurious correlation problems. In particular, when the first differences correction is used to correct for
nonstationarity detected in the underlying data series, the results of the original paper are overturned.

14. Other studies analyze the impact of development programs on voters' behav-
iors and political outcomes of incumbent candidates, which can be associated
with civilian attitudes toward the government. These studies largely suggest
that development programs provide political gains to governments when
incumbent parties rerun in elections (De La O 2013; Labonne 2013;
Manacorda, Miguel, and Vigorito 2011).

15. See Bazzi and Clemens (2013) for a critique of the capacity of the instruments
used in these studies to correct for endogeneity.

16. Assuming that A is large enough, the optimal solution gives positive payoffs
to both players, so that the first-order condition is also sufficient.

References

Ahmed, F. Z. 2016. "Does Foreign Aid Harm Political Rights? Evidence from
US Aid." *Quarterly Journal of Political Science* 11 (2): 83–217.

Ahn, D. P., and R. D. Ludema. 2019. "The Sword and the Shield: The Economics
of Targeted Sanctions." CESifo Working Paper 7620, CESifo Group, Munich.

Akerlof, G., and J. Yellen. 1994. "Gang Behavior, Law Enforcement, and
Community Values." In *Values and Public Policy*, edited by H. Aaron, T. Mann,
and T. Taylor, 173–209. Washington, DC: Brookings Institution Press.

Alesina, A., and B. Weder. 2002. "Do Corrupt Governments Receive Less Foreign
Aid?" *American Economic Review* 92 (4): 1126–37.

Allen, S. H., and D. J. Lektzian. 2013. "Economic Sanctions: A Blunt Instrument?"
Journal of Peace Research 50 (1): 121–35.

Andrabi, T., and J. Das. 2017. "In Aid We Trust: Hearts and Minds and the Pakistan
Earthquake of 2005." *Review of Economics and Statistics* 99 (3): 371–86.

Armand, A., P. Atwell, and J. Gomes. 2017. "The Reach of Radio: Defection
Messaging and Armed Group Behavior." HiCN Working Papers 249,
Households in Conflict Network, Brighton, UK.

Armand, A., A. Coutts, P. C. Vicente, and I. Vilela. 2019. "Does Information
Break the Political Resource Curse? Experimental Evidence from
Mozambique." NCID Working Papers 01/2019, Navarra Center for
International Development, University of Navarra, Pamplona, Spain.

Asher, S., and P. Novosad. 2019. "Rent-Seeking and Criminal Politicians: Evidence from Mining Booms." Working paper.

Autor, D. H., D. Dorn, and G. H. Hanson. 2013. "The China Syndrome: Local Labor Market Effects of Import Competition in the United States." *American Economic Review* 103 (6): 2121–68.

Avdeenko, A., and M. J. Gilligan. 2015. "International Interventions to Build Social Capital: Evidence from a Field Experiment in Sudan." *American Political Science Review* 109 (2): 427–49.

Axbard, S., J. Poulsen, and A. Tolonen. 2016. "Extractive Industries, Production Shocks and Criminality: Evidence from a Middle-Income Country." CDEP-CGEG Working Paper 30, Center for Development Economics and Policy, Columbia University, New York.

Azam, J.-P., and A. Delacroix. 2006. "Aid and the Delegated Fight against Terrorism." *Review of Development Economics* 10 (2): 330–44.

Azam, J.-P., and A. Hoeffler. 2002. "Violence against Civilians in Civil Wars: Looting or Terror?" *Journal of Peace Research* 39 (4): 461–85.

Azam, J.-P., and V. Thelen. 2010a. "Foreign Aid versus Military Intervention in the War on Terror." *Journal of Conflict Resolution* 54 (2): 237–61.

———. 2010b. "The Roles of Foreign Aid and Education in the War on Terror." *Public Choice* 135 (3): 375–97.

Baliga, S., and T. Sjöström. 2004. "Arms Races and Negotiations." *Review of Economic Studies* 71 (2): 351–69.

Bapat, N. A. 2011. "Transnational Terrorism, US Military Aid, and the Incentive to Misrepresent." *Journal of Peace Research* 48 (3): 303–18.

Bara, C. 2018. "Legacies of Violence: Conflict-Specific Capital and the Postconflict Diffusion of Civil War." *Journal of Conflict Resolution* 62 (9): 1991–2016.

Barr, R., and K. Pease. 1990. "Crime Placement, Displacement, and Deflection." In *Crime and Justice: A Review of Research*, vol. 12, edited by M. Tonry and N. Morris, 277–318. Chicago: University of Chicago Press.

Bartlett, B. L., and D. Ballantine. 2002. "The Negative Effects of Money Laundering on Economic Development." Asian Development Bank Regional Technical Assistance Project 5967: Countering Money Laundering in the Asian and Pacific Region, ADB, Manila, Philippines.

Bazzi, S., and C. Blattman. 2014. "Economic Shocks and Conflict: Evidence from Commodity Prices." *American Economic Journal: Macroeconomics* 6 (4): 1–38.

Bazzi, S., and M. Clemens. 2013. "Blunt Instruments: Avoiding Common Pitfalls in Identifying the Causes of Economic Growth." *American Economic Journal: Macroeconomics* 5 (2): 152–86.

Beardsley, K. 2011. "Peacekeeping and the Contagion of Armed Conflict." *Journal of Politics* 73 (4): 1051–64.

Beath, A., C. Fotini, and R. Enikolopov. 2012. "Winning Hearts and Minds through Development: Evidence from a Field Experiment in Afghanistan." Policy Research Working Paper 6129, World Bank, Washington, DC.

Berman, E., J. H. Felter, J. N. Shapiro, and E. Troland. 2013. "Modest, Secure and Informed: Successful Development in Conflict Zones." *American Economic Review* 103 (3): 512–17.

Berman, E., J. N. Shapiro, and J. H. Felter. 2011. "Can Hearts and Minds Be Bought? The Economics of Counterinsurgency in Iraq." *Journal of Political Economy* 119 (4): 766–819.

Berman, N., and M. Couttenier. 2015. "External Shocks, Internal Shots: The Geography of Civil Conflicts." *Review of Economics and Statistics* 97 (4): 758–76.

Berman, N., M. Couttenier, D. Rohner, and M. Thoenig. 2017. "This Mine Is Mine! How Minerals Fuel Conflicts in Africa." *American Economic Review* 107 (6): 1564–610.

Besley, T., and M. Ghatak. 2005. "Competition and Incentives with Motivated Agents." *American Economic Review* 95 (3): 616–36.

Besley, T., and T. Persson. 2011. "Fragile States and Development Policy." *Journal of the European Economic Association* 9 (3): 371–98.

Black, N. 2013. "When Have Violent Civil Conflicts Spread? Introducing a Dataset of Substate Conflict Contagion." *Journal of Peace Research* 50 (6): 751–59.

Blair, G., K. Imai, and J. Lyall. 2014. "Comparing and Combining List and Endorsement Experiments: Evidence from Afghanistan." *American Journal of Political Science* 58 (4): 1043–63.

Blattman, C., and J. Annan. 2016. "Can Employment Reduce Lawlessness and Rebellion? A Field Experiment with High-Risk Men in a Fragile State." *American Political Science Review* 110 (1): 1–17.

Blattman, C., D. P. Green, D. Ortega, and S. Tobon. 2019. "Place-Based Interventions at Scale: The Direct and Spillover Effects of Policing and City Services on Crime." Working Paper 2019-40, Becker Friedman Institute, Chicago.

Blattman, C., and E. Miguel. 2010. "Civil War." *Journal of Economic Literature* 48 (1): 3–57.

Blouin, A. T., and S. W. Mukand. 2019. "Erasing Ethnicity? Propaganda, Nation Building and Identity in Rwanda." *Journal of Political Economy* 127 (3): 1008–62.

Böhnke, J. R., and C. Zürcher. 2013. "Aid, Minds and Hearts: The Impact of Aid in Conflict Zones." *Conflict Management and Peace Science* 30 (5): 411–32.

Braga, A. A., D. L. Weisburd, E. J. Waring, L. G. Mazerolle, W. Spelman, and F. Gajewski. 1999. "Problem-Oriented Policing in Violent Crime Places: A Randomized Controlled Experiment." *Criminology* 37 (3): 541–80.

Braithwaite, A. 2010. "Resisting Infection: How State Capacity Conditions Conflict Contagion." *Journal of Peace Research* 47 (3): 311–19.

Brückner, M., and A. Ciccone. 2010. "International Commodity Prices, Growth and the Outbreak of Civil War in Sub-Saharan Africa." *Economic Journal* 120 (544): 519–34.

Buhaug, H., and K. S. Gleditsch. 2008. "Contagion or Confusion? Why Conflicts Cluster in Space." *International Studies Quarterly* 52 (2): 215–33.

Burnside, C., and D. Dollar. 2000. "Aid, Policies, and Growth." *American Economic Review* 90 (34): 847–68.

Casey, K., R. Glennerster, and E. Miguel. 2012. "Reshaping Institutions: Evidence on Aid Impacts Using a Preanalysis Plan." *Quarterly Journal of Economics* 127 (4): 1755–812.

Chassang, S., and G. Padró i Miquel. 2010. "Conflict and Deterrence under Strategic Risk." *Quarterly Journal of Economics* 125 (4): 1821–58.

Chenoweth, E., and A. Lawrence. 2010. *Rethinking Violence: States and Non-State Actors in Conflict.* Cambridge, MA: MIT University Press.

Child, T. B. 2018. "Conflict and Counterinsurgency Aid: Drawing Sectoral Distinctions." *Journal of Development Economics* 141 (November): 1–13.

Chou, T. 2012. "Does Development Assistance Reduce Violence? Evidence from Afghanistan." *Economics of Peace and Security Journal* 7 (2): 5–13.

Christensen, D. 2019. "Concession Stands: How Mining Investments Incite Protest in Africa." *International Organization* 73 (1): 65–101.

Christian, P., and C. Barrett. 2017. "Revisiting the Effect of Food Aid on Conflict: A Methodological Caution." Policy Research Working Paper 8171, World Bank, Washington, DC.

Cilliers, J., O. Dube, and B. Siddiqi. 2016. "Reconciling after Civil Conflict Increases Social Capital but Decreases Individual Well-Being." *Science* 352 (6287): 787–94.

Clarke, R. V., and D. Weisburd. 1994. "Diffusion of Crime Control Benefits: Observations on the Reverse of Displacement." *Crime Prevention Studies* 2: 165–84.

Collier, P., and A. Hoeffler. 1998. "On Economic Causes of Civil War." *Oxford Economic Papers* 50 (4): 563–73.

———. 2002. "Aid, Policy and Peace: Reducing the Risks of Civil Conflict." *Defence and Peace Economics* 13 (6): 435–50.

———. 2004. "Greed and Grievance in Civil War." *Oxford Economic Papers* 56 (4): 563–95.

Condra, L. N., J. D. Long, A. C. Shaver, and A. L. Wright. 2018. "The Logic of Insurgent Electoral Violence." *American Economic Review* 108 (1): 3199–231.

Condra, L. N., and J. Shapiro. 2012. "Who Takes the Blame? The Strategic Effects of Collateral Damage." *American Journal of Political Science* 56 (1): 167–87.

Crost, B., J. Felter, and P. B. Johnston. 2014. "Aid under Fire: Development Projects and Civil Conflict." *American Economic Review* 104 (6): 1833–56.

———. 2016. "Conditional Cash Transfers, Civil Conflict and Insurgent Influence: Experimental Evidence from the Philippines." *Journal of Development Economics* 118 (C): 171–82.

Cunningham, D. E. 2006. "Veto Players and Civil War Duration." *American Journal of Political Science* 50 (4): 875–92.

Cunningham, S., and M. Shah. 2018. "Decriminalizing Indoor Prostitution: Implications for Sexual Violence and Public Health." *Review of Economic Studies* 85 (3): 1683–715.

Dal Bó, E., and R. Powell. 2009. "A Model of Spoils Politics." *American Journal of Political Science* 53 (1): 207–22.

De La O, A. L. 2013. "Do Conditional Cash Transfers Affect Electoral Behavior? Evidence from a Randomized Experiment in Mexico." *American Journal of Political Science* 57 (1): 1–14.

De Ree, J., and E. Nillesen. 2009. "Aiding Violence or Peace? The Impact of Foreign Aid on the Risk of Civil Conflict in Sub-Saharan Africa." *Journal of Development Economics* 88 (2): 301–13.

Dell, M., B. Feigenberg, and K. Teshima. 2019. "The Violent Consequences of Trade-Induced Worker Displacement in Mexico." *American Economic Review: Insights* 1 (1): 43–58.

Dell, M., and P. Querubin. 2018. "Nation Building through Foreign Intervention: Evidence from Discontinuities in Military Strategies." *Quarterly Journal of Economics* 133 (2): 701–64.

Della Vigna, S., R. Enikolopov, V. Mironova, M. Petrova, and E. Zhuravskaya. 2014. "Cross-Border Media and Nationalism: Evidence from Serbian Radio in Croatia." *American Economic Journal: Applied Economics* 6 (3): 103–32.

Di Tella, R., and E. Schargrodsky. 2004. "Do Police Reduce Crime? Estimates Using the Allocation of Police Forces after a Terrorist Attack." *American Economic Review* 94 (1): 115–33.

Dills, A. K., J. A. Miron, and G. Summers. 2010. "What Do Economists Know about Crime?" In *The Economics of Crime: Lessons for and from Latin America*, edited by R. Di Tella, S. Edwards, and E. Schargrodsky, 269–304. Chicago: University of Chicago Press.

Dix-Carneiro, R., R. R. Soares, and G. Ulyssea. 2018. "Economic Shocks and Crime: Evidence from the Brazilian Trade Liberalization." *American Economic Journal: Applied Economics* 10 (4): 158–95.

Dixit, A. 1987. "Strategic Behavior in Contests." *American Economic Review* 77 (5): 891–98.

Djankov, S., J. G. Montalvo, and M. Reynal-Querol. 2008. "The Curse of Aid." *Journal of Economic Growth* 13 (3): 169–94.

Do, Q.-T., A. A. Levchenko, L. Ma, J. Blanc, H. Dublin, and T. Milliken. 2018. "The Price Elasticity of African Elephant Poaching." Policy Research Working Paper 8335, World Bank, Washington, DC.

Do, Q.-T., L. Ma, and C. Ruiz. 2016. "Pirates of Somalia: Crime and Deterrence on the High Seas." Policy Research Working Paper 7757, World Bank, Washington, DC.

Draca, M., and S. Machin. 2015. "Crime and Economic Incentives." *Annual Review of Economics* 7 (1): 389–408.

Draca, M., S. Machin, and R. Witt. 2011. "Panic on the Streets of London: Police, Crime, and the July 2005 Terror Attacks." *American Economic Review* 101 (5): 2157–81.

Dube, A., O. Dube, and O. García-Ponce. 2013. "Cross-Border Spillover: US Gun Laws and Violence in Mexico." *American Political Science Review* 107 (3): 397–417.

Dube, O., and J. F. Vargas. 2013. "Commodity Price Shocks and Civil Conflict: Evidence from Colombia." *Review of Economic Studies* 80 (4): 1384–421.

Easterly, W. 2003. "Can Foreign Aid Buy Growth?" *Journal of Economic Perspectives* 17 (3): 23–48.

Enikolopov, R., A. Makarin, and M. Petrova. 2018. "Social Media and Protest Participation: Evidence from Russia." CEPR Discussion Papers 11254, Center for Economic and Policy Research, Washington, DC.

Escribà-Folch, A. 2010. "Economic Sanctions and the Duration of Civil Conflicts." *Journal of Peace Research* 47 (2): 129–41.

Esteban, J., and D. Ray. 2001. "Collective Action and the Group Size Paradox." *American Political Science Review* 95 (3): 663–72.

———. 2011. "A Model of Ethnic Conflict." *Journal of the European Economic Association* 9 (3): 496–521.

Fajnzylber, P., D. Lederman, and N. Loayza. 2002a. "Inequality and Violent Crime." *Journal of Law and Economics* 45 (1): 1–40.

———. 2002b. "What Causes Violent Crime?" *European Economic Review* 46 (7): 1323–56.

FATF (Financial Action Task Force). 2019. "International Standards on Combating Money Laundering and the Financing of Terrorism and Proliferation: The FATF Recommendations." FATF, Paris.

Fearon, J. D. 1995. "Rationalist Explanations for War." *International Organization* 49 (3): 379–414.

———. 2004. "Why Do Some Civil Wars Last So Much Longer Than Others?" *Journal of Peace Research* 41 (3): 275–301.

———. 2008. "Economic Development, Insurgency and Civil War." In *Institutions and Economic Performance*, edited by Elhanan Helpman, 292–328. Cambridge, MA: Harvard University Press.

Fearon, J., M. Humphreys, and J. Weinstein. 2009. "Can Development Aid Contribute to Social Cohesion after Civil War? Evidence from a Field Experiment in Post-Conflict Liberia." *American Economic Review: Papers and Proceedings* 99 (2): 287–91.

———. 2015. "How Does Development Assistance Affect Collective Action Capacity? Results from a Field Experiment in Post-Conflict Liberia." *American Political Science Review* 109 (3): 450–69.

Forsberg, E. 2008. "Polarization and Ethnic Conflict in a Widened Strategic Setting." *Journal of Peace Research* 45 (2): 283–300.

———. 2014. "Transnational Transmitters: Ethnic Kinship Ties and Conflict Contagion, 1946–2009." *International Interactions* 40 (2): 143–65.

Fox, J. 2004. "The Rise of Religious Nationalism and Conflict: Ethnic Conflict and Revolutionary Wars, 1945–2001." *Journal of Peace Research* 41 (6): 715–31.

Frankel, J. A., and D. H. Romer. 1999. "Does Trade Cause Growth?" *American Economic Review* 89 (3): 379–99.

Galiani, S., S. Knack, L. C. Xu, and B. Zou. 2017. "The Effect of Aid on Growth: Evidence from a Quasi-Experiment." *Journal of Economic Growth* 22 (1): 1–33.

Garfinkel, M. R. 1990. "Arming as a Strategic Investment in a Cooperative Equilibrium." *American Economic Review* 80 (1): 50–68.

Garfinkel, M. R., and I. S. Skaperdas. 2007. "Economics of Conflict: An Overview." Chapter 22 in *Handbook of Defense Economics*, Vol. 2, edited by K. Hartley and T. Sandler, 649–709. New York: Oxford University Press.

———. 2012. *The Oxford Handbook of the Economics of Peace and Conflict*. Oxford, UK: Oxford University Press.

Gavrilova, E., T. Kamada, and F. Zoutman. 2017. "Is Legal Pot Crippling Mexican Drug Trafficking Organisations? The Effect of Medical Marijuana Laws on US Crime." *Economic Journal* 129 (617): 375–407.

Gilligan, M. J., E. N. Mvukiyehe, and C. Samii. 2012. "Reintegrating Rebels into Civilian Life: Quasi-Experimental Evidence from Burundi." *Journal of Conflict Resolution* 57 (4): 598–626.

Gleditsch, K. S., I. Salehyan, and K. Schultz. 2008. "Fighting at Home, Fighting Abroad: How Civil Wars Lead to International Disputes." *Journal of Conflict Resolution* 52 (40): 479–506.

Goldberg, P. K. 2015. "Introduction." In *Trade and Inequality*, edited by P. K. Goldberg. International Library of Critical Writings in Economics Series. Cheltenham, UK: Edward Elgar.

Grossman, H. I. 1999. "Kleptocracy and Revolutions." *Oxford Economic Papers* 51 (2): 267–83.

Haavelmo, T. 2015. "Structural Models and Econometrics." *Econometric Theory* 31 (1): 85–92.

Hammarström, M. 1994. "The Diffusion of Military Conflict: Central and South-East Europe in 1919–20 and 1991–92." *Journal of Peace Research* 31 (3): 263–80.

Helpman, E., O. Itskhoki, M.-A. Muendler, and S. J. Redding. 2017. "Trade and Inequality: From Theory to Estimation." *Review of Economic Studies* 84 (1): 357–405.

Hirshleifer, J. 1989. "Conflict and Rent-Seeking Success Functions: Ratio vs. Difference Models of Relative Success." *Public Choice* 63 (2): 101–12.

Hultman, L., and D. Peksen. 2017. "Successful or Counterproductive Coercion? The Effect of International Sanctions on Conflict Intensity." *Journal of Conflict Resolution* 61 (6): 1315–39.

Humphreys, M., and J. M. Weinstein. 2008. "Who Fights? The Determinants of Participation in Civil War." *American Journal of Political Science* 52 (2): 436–55.

Iyer, L., and P. B. Topalova. 2014. "Poverty and Crime: Evidence from Rainfall and Trade Shocks in India." Harvard Business School BGIE Unit Working Paper 14-067, Harvard Business School, Cambridge, MA.

Jackson, M. O., and M. Morelli. 2007. "Political Bias and War." *American Economic Review* 97 (4): 1353–73.

Jacob, B., L. Lefgren, and E. Moretti. 2004. "The Dynamics of Criminal Behavior: Evidence from Weather Shocks." NBER Working Paper 10739, National Bureau of Economic Research, Cambridge, MA.

Jia, H., and S. Skaperdas. 2012. "Technologies of Conflict." In *Handbook of the Economics of Peace and Conflict*, edited by M. R. Garfinkel and S. Skaperdas, 449–72. New York: Oxford University Press.

Johnston, P. B., and A. K. Sarbahi. 2016. "The Impact of US Drone Strikes on Terrorism in Pakistan." *International Studies Quarterly* 60 (2): 203–19.

Jordan, J. 2009. "When Heads Roll: Assessing the Effectiveness of Leadership Decapitation." *Security Studies* 18 (4): 719–55.

Kalyvas, S. N. 2006. *The Logic of Violence in Civil War*. Cambridge Studies in Comparative Politics. Cambridge, UK: Cambridge University Press.

Kalyvas, S. N., and M. A. Kocher. 2009. "The Dynamics of Violence in Vietnam: An Analysis of the Hamlet Evaluation System (HES)." *Journal of Peace Research* 46 (3): 335–55.

Kathman, J. D. 2010. "Civil War Contagion and Neighboring Interventions." *International Studies Quarterly* 54 (4): 989–1012.

———. 2011. "Civil War Diffusion and Regional Motivations for Intervention." *Journal of Conflict Resolution* 55 (6): 847–76.

Khanna, G., and L. Zimmermann. 2014. "Fighting Maoist Violence with Promises: Evidence from India's Employment Guarantee Scheme." *Economic Peace Security Journal* 9 (1): 30–36.

———. 2017. "Guns and Butter? Fighting Violence with the Promise of Development." *Journal of Development Economics* 124 (1): 120–41.

Knight, B. 2013. "State Gun Policy and Cross-State Externalities: Evidence from Crime Gun Tracing." *American Economic Journal: Economic Policy* 5 (4): 200–29.

Kocher, M. A., T. B. Pepinsky, and S. N. Kalyvas. 2011. "Aerial Bombing and Counterinsurgency in the Vietnam War." *American Journal of Political Science* 55 (2): 201–18.

Konrad, K. A. 2009. *Strategy and Dynamics in Contests.* New York: Oxford University Press.

Krueger, A. B., and D. Laitin. 2008. "Kto Kogo? A Cross-Country Study of the Origins and Targets of Terrorism." In *Terrorism, Economic Development, and Political Openness*, edited by P. Keefer and N. Loaya, 148–73. New York: Cambridge University Press.

Krueger, A. B., and J. Malečková. 2009. "Attitudes and Action: Public Opinion and the Occurrence of International Terrorism." *Science* 325 (5947): 1534–36.

Labonne, J. 2013. "The Local Electoral Impact of Conditional Cash Transfers: Evidence from a Field Experiment." *Journal of Development Economics* 104: 73–88.

Lazear, E., and S. Rosen. 1981. "Rank-Order Tournaments as Optimum Labor Contracts." *Journal of Political Economy* 89 (5): 841–64.

Leeson, P. 2009. *The Invisible Hook: The Hidden Economics of Pirates.* Princeton, NJ: Princeton University Press.

Lektzian, D., and P. M. Regan. 2016. "Economic Sanctions, Military Interventions, and Civil Conflict Outcomes." *Journal of Peace Research* 53 (4): 554–68.

Luce, R. D. 1959. *Individual Choice Behavior.* Oxford, UK: John Wiley.

Lyall, J. 2019. "Civilian Casualties, Humanitarian Aid, and Insurgent Violence in Civil Wars." *International Organization* 73 (4): 901–26.

Manacorda, M., E. Miguel, and A. Vigorito. 2011. "Government Transfers and Political Support." *American Economic Journal: Applied Economics* 3 (3): 1–28.

Manacorda, M., and A. Tesei. 2016. "Liberation Technology: Mobile Phones and Political Mobilization in Africa." CESifo Working Paper 5904, Center for Economic Studies, Munich.

Marinov, N. 2005. "Do Economic Sanctions Destabilize Country Leaders?" *American Journal of Political Science* 49 (3): 564–76.

Maves, J., and A. Braithwaite. 2013. "Autocratic Institutions and Civil Conflict Contagion." *Journal of Politics* 75 (2): 478–90.

McFadden, D. 1973. "Conditional Logit Analysis of Qualitative Choice Behavior." In *Frontiers in Econometrics*, edited by P. Zarembka, 105–42. New York: Academic Press.

McGuirk, E., and M. Burke. 2018. "The Economic Origins of Conflict in Africa." NBER Working Paper 23056, National Bureau of Economic Research, Cambridge, MA.

Mir, A., and D. Moore. 2018. "Drones, Surveillance, and Violence: Theory and Evidence from a US Drone Program." *International Studies Quarterly* 43 (2): 45–83.

Miron, J. A. 2003. "The Effect of Drug Prohibition on Drug Prices: Evidence from the Markets for Cocaine and Heroin." *Review of Economics and Statistics* 85 (3): 522–30.

Most, B. A., and H. Starr. 1980. "Diffusion, Reinforcement, Geopolitics, and the Spread of War." *American Political Science Review* 74 (4): 932–46.

———. 1983. "Conceptualizing 'War': Consequences for Theory and Research." *Journal of Conflict Resolution* 27 (1): 137–59.

Murdoch, J. C., and T. Sandler. 2002. "Economic Growth, Civil Wars, and Spatial Spillovers." *Journal of Conflict Resolution* 46 (1): 91–110.

———. 2004. "Civil Wars and Economic Growth: Spatial Dispersion." *American Journal of Political Science* 48 (1): 138–51.

Narang, N. 2014. "Humanitarian Assistance and the Duration of Peace after Civil War." *Journal of Politics* 76 (2): 446–60.

———. 2015. "Assisting Uncertainty: How Humanitarian Aid Can Inadvertently Prolong Civil War." *International Studies Quarterly* 59 (1): 184–95.

Narang, N., and J. A. Stanton. 2017. "A Strategic Logic of Attacking Aid Workers: Evidence from Violence in Afghanistan." *International Studies Quarterly* 61 (1): 38–51.

Neuenkirch, M., and F. Neumeier. 2015. "The Impact of UN and US Economic Sanctions on GDP Growth." *European Journal of Political Economy* 40 (A): 110–25.

Nunn, N., and N. Qian. 2014. "US Food Aid and Civil Conflict." *American Economic Review* 104 (6): 1630–66.

Osorio, J. 2015. "The Contagion of Drug Violence: Spatiotemporal Dynamics of the Mexican War on Drugs." *Journal of Conflict Resolution* 59 (8): 1403–32.

Paluck, E. L. 2009. "Reducing Intergroup Prejudice and Conflict with the Media: A Field Experiment in Rwanda." *Journal of Personality and Social Psychology* 96 (3): 574–87.

Peksen, D. 2009. "Better or Worse? The Effect of Economic Sanctions on Human Rights." *Journal of Peace Research* 46 (1): 59–77.

Powell, R. 2006. "War as a Commitment Problem." *International Organization* 60 (2): 169–203.

Prendergast, C. 2007. "The Motivation and Bias of Bureaucrats." *American Economic Review* 97 (1): 180–96.

———. 2008. "Intrinsic Motivation and Incentives." *American Economic Review* 98 (2): 201–05.

Price, B. C. 2012. "Targeting Top Terrorists: How Leadership Decapitation Contributes to Counterterrorism." *International Security* 36 (4): 9–46.

Qian, N. 2015. "Making Progress on Foreign Aid." *Annual Review of Economics* 7 (1): 277–308.

Rajan, R., and A. Subramanian. 2007. "Does Aid Affect Governance?" *American Economic Review* 97 (2): 322–27.

Regan, P. M. 2002. "Third-Party Interventions and the Duration of Intrastate Conflicts." *Journal of Conflict Resolution* 46 (1): 55–73.

Reppetto, T. A. 1976. "Crime Prevention and the Displacement Phenomenon." *Crime and Delinquency* 22 (2): 166–77.

Ross, M. L. 2004a. "What Do We Know about Natural Resources and Civil War?" *Journal of Peace Research* 41 (3): 337–56.

———. 2004b. "How Do Natural Resources Influence Civil War? Evidence from Thirteen Cases." *International Organization* 58 (1): 35–67.

Salehyan, I., and K. S. Gleditsch. 2006. "Refugees and the Spread of Civil War." *International Organization* 60 (2): 335–66.

Sexton, R. 2019. "Unpacking the Local Resource Curse: How Externalities and Governance Shape Social Conflict." *Journal of Conflict Resolution*, September 12, https://journals.sagepub.com/doi/10.1177/0022002719873044.

Shapiro, J., and N. Weidmann. 2015. "Is the Phone Mightier Than the Sword? Cell Phones and Insurgent Violence in Iraq." *International Organization* 69 (2): 247–74.

Shaver, A., and J. Shapiro. Forthcoming. "The Effect of Civilian Casualties on Wartime Informing: New Evidence from Iraq." *Journal of Conflict Resolution*.

Sherman, L., and D. Rogan. 1995. "Effects of Gun Seizures on Gun Violence: 'Hot Spots' Patrol in Kansas City." *Justice Quarterly* 12 (4): 673–94.

Siverson, R. M., and H. Starr. 1990. "Opportunity, Willingness, and the Diffusion of War." *American Political Science Review* 84 (1): 47–67.

Skaperdas, S. 1992. "Cooperation, Conflict, and Power in the Absence of Property Rights." *American Economic Review* 82 (4): 720–39.

———. 1996. "Contest Success Functions." *Economic Theory* 7 (2): 283–90.

Soares, L. E. 2006. "Segurança Pública: Presente e Future [Public Security: Present and Future]." *Estudos Avançados* 20 (56): 91–106.

Stremlau, J. 1996. "Sharpening International Sanctions: Toward a Stronger Role for the United Nations." A report to the Carnegie Commission on Preventing Deadly Conflict, Carnegie Corporation of New York.

Sunstein, C. R. 1996. "On the Expressive Function of Law." *University of Pennsylvania Law Review* 144 (5): 2021–53.

Szymanski, S. 2003. "The Economic Design of Sporting Contests." *Journal of Economic Literature* 41 (4): 1137–87.

Tavares, J. 2003. "Does Foreign Aid Corrupt?" *Economic Letters* 79 (1): 99–106.

Tullock, G. 1980. "Efficient Rent-Seeking." In *Toward a Theory of a Rent-Seeking Society*, edited by J. Buchanan, R. Tollison, and G. Tullock, 97–112. College Station, TX: Texas A&M University Press.

UNODC (United Nations Office on Drugs and Crime). 2011a. *The Globalization of Crime: A Transnational Organized Crime Threat Assessment*. Vienna: UNODC.

———. 2011b. *The Global Afghan Opium Trade: A Threat Assessment*. Vienna: UNODC.

———. 2017. *The Drug Problem and Organized Crime, Illicit Financial Flows, Corruption and Terrorism*. Part 5 of *The World Drug Report 2017*. Vienna: UNODC.

Verdugo Yepes, C. 2011. "Compliance with the AML/CFT International Standard: Lessons from a Cross-Country Analysis." IMF Working Paper 11/177, International Monetary Fund, Washington, DC.

Vigne, L., and E. Martin. 2017. *Decline in the Legal Ivory Trade in China in Anticipation of a Ban.* Nairobi: Save the Elephants.

Weintraub, M. 2016. "Do All Good Things Go Together? Development Assistance and Violence in Insurgency." *Journal of Politics* 78 (4): 989–1002.

Weisburd, D., and L. Green. 1995. "Policing Drug Hot Spots: The Jersey City DMA Experiment." *Justice Quarterly* 12 (4): 711–36.

Weisburd, D., L. A. Wyckoff, J. Ready, J. E. Eck, J. C. Hinkle, and F. Gajewski. 2006. "Does Crime Just Move around the Corner? A Controlled Study of Spatial Displacement and Diffusion of Crime Control Benefits." *Criminology* 44 (3): 549–92.

Weiss, T. G. 1999. "Principles, Politics, and Humanitarian Action." *Ethics and International Affairs* 13 (1): 1–22.

Wood, E. J. 2008. "The Social Processes of Civil War: The Wartime Transformation of Social Networks." *Annual Review of Political Science* 11 (1): 539–61.

Wood, R. M. 2010. "Rebel Capability and Strategic Violence against Civilians." *Journal of Peace Research* 47 (5): 601–14.

Wood, R. M., and C. Sullivan. 2015. "Doing Harm by Doing Good? The Negative Externalities of Humanitarian Aid Provision during Civil Conflict." *Journal of Politics* 77 (3): 736–48.

World Bank. 2016. *Making Politics Work for Development: Harnessing Transparency and Citizen Engagement.* Washington, DC: World Bank.

Wright, A. L. 2016. "Economic Shocks and Rebel Tactics." HiCN Working Paper 232, Households in Conflict Network, Brighton, UK.

Yanagizawa-Drott, D. 2014. "Propaganda and Conflict: Evidence from the Rwandan Genocide." *Quarterly Journal of Economics* 129 (4): 1947–94.

Young, J. K., and M. G. Findley. 2011. "Can Peace Be Purchased? A Sectoral-Level Analysis of Aid's Influence on Transnational Terrorism." *Public Choice* 149 (December): 365–81.

Zhukov, Y. M. 2016. "Trading Hard Hats for Combat Helmets: The Economics of Rebellion in Eastern Ukraine." *Journal of Comparative Economics* 44 (1): 1–15.

Zürcher, C. 2017. "What Do We (Not) Know about Development Aid and Violence? A Systematic Review." *World Development* 98 (C): 506–22.

CHAPTER 3

Security in a Globalized World

Global market integration implies, this report has argued, that countries have an increased stake in each other's fate. This final chapter discusses what country interdependence means in terms of international interactions. The chapter's main focus will be on the different roles that other countries and multilateral institutions can play in mitigating internal conflict, crime, or violence.

Countries often use humanitarian or development assistance or military interventions to intervene in other countries. As shown, the actual drivers of such involvement can diverge significantly from those needed for maximum effectiveness. Delegation of aspects of a country's foreign policy to a multilateral institution or international agency constitutes one response to the collective action problem underlying private provision of global security; however, delegation comes with its own limitations.

The report concludes with a set of recommendations that include (1) a call for more and better data for research and policy analyses, (2) upholding the "do-no-harm" principle while providing assistance to countries implementing policies targeted toward reducing internal conflict and crime, and (3) outlining the role of multilateral institutions and international agencies in the provision of security as a regional and global public good.

Third-party interventions to prevent violence

International third-party intermediation can prevent violence by, for example, changing the parameters of the contest success function (opportunity costs, value of the prize), resolving information asymmetries, and mitigating commitment problems. The internationalization of these events means that domestic political stability and law enforcement capacity are regional, or even global, public goods. From a public economics perspective, fragile countries are thus candidates for support, a "Pigouvian" subsidy, to maintain peace and enforce the rule of law.[1] Foreign assistance becomes all the more relevant when countries face more stringent fiscal constraints. The previous chapter reviewed a number of studies on the effects of aid and military interventions on the different drivers of conflict. This section takes stock of other ways in which third parties can be effective in reducing conflict and crime, and it discusses the trends in such interventions.

Conflict prevention tools include adopting inclusive policies, establishing early warning systems, preventive diplomacy, and mediation and peacekeeping missions. These tools can be more cost-effective than interventions after conflicts start (United Nations and World Bank 2018). International bodies like the United Nations (UN) Security Council, while restricted by political barriers, can still take a proactive stance in preventing conflict (White, Cunningham, and Beardsley 2018).

One key role for third parties is to reduce the information asymmetries between opposing groups that are aiming for peaceful resolutions. As the previous chapter reviewed, the lack of verifiable information on the costs, benefits, and actions faced by the other party can be a significant deterrent to peacebuilding. When peace is reached through several simultaneous demilitarization steps undertaken by both parties, such actions must be verifiable, and a third party can provide that service. In interstate conflict, for example, UN agencies like the International Atomic Energy Agency have a clear mandate to provide verifiable information on a country's nuclear programs.

The role of a third party in peace agreements is also evident when parties are unable to commit to a cease-fire or to an agreed division of resources. Once a peace deal is approved and steps are taken toward peace, any change in the balance of power between the parties will lead to a renegotiation of part of the deal through, for example, the resumption of hostilities (Walter 2002). Inability of parties to commit to a cease-fire restricts agreements to those that are renegotiation-proof. A third party can fill this void; peacekeeping forces can be viewed as a means to constrain the parties to commit to a cease-fire. The incipient empirical literature suggests that diplomacy that addresses disputes early on reduces the likelihood of armed conflict (Beardsley, Cunningham, and White 2017). Membership in international clubs that have coercive capacity and the

Figure 3.1 Trends in United Nations peacekeeping operations and global aid flows, 1947–2017

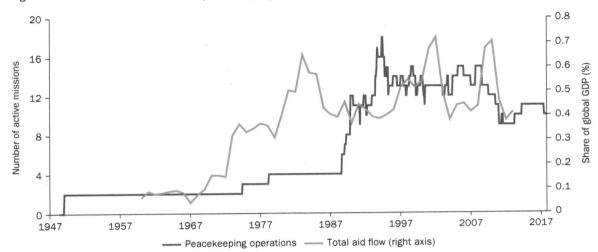

Sources: AidData Core Research Release, version 3.1, https://www.aiddata.org/data/aiddata-core-research-release-level-1-3-1; AidData Global Chinese Official Finance Dataset, 2000–14, version 1.0, https://www.aiddata.org/data/chinese-global-official-finance-dataset; United Nations Department of Peace Operations, Global Peacekeeping data (2019), https://peacekeeping.un.org/en/data.

means to enforce decisions can prevent conflict by increasing the costs of escalation, thereby providing incentives for settlement and reducing bargaining failures (Karreth and Tir 2013).

Figure 3.1 shows trends in global aid flows and peacekeeping operations over the period 1947–2017. The current number of active missions is 10, whereas the historical high was 18 during May and June of 1994. Global aid flows stood at 0.4 percent of global gross domestic product (GDP) in 2013 (latest available data), lower than the historical high of 0.7 percent attained during the early 2000s.

When will other countries intervene in conflict situations?

Where cross-border spillovers occur, mitigation of conflict, crime, and violence can be seen as a global or regional public good. Because donor countries are sovereign entities, however, provision of global security is subject to country voluntary contributions. The proponents of the neo-realist view of international relations would predict that, without any supranational institution regulating individual country behavior, global security would be underprovided, with each country acting in its own self-interest (see, for example, Brooks and Wohlforth 2008). Individual country decisions may thus be subject to the free-rider problem and result in underprovision of investments to global security. Such inefficiencies have been documented in the extensive literature on the private provision of public goods (see, for example, Bergström, Blume, and Varian 1986 and a review in Fudenberg and Tirole 1991). This section reviews the evidence on individual country motivations to engage in third-party interventions.

Strategic motivations for development assistance

The collective action problem might find an efficient solution when the parties have a private interest in the outcome of conflict or crime. Beyond pure altruistic motivations such as reducing global poverty, the literature points to strategic reasons for development assistance (McKinlay 2006; McKinlay and Little 1977, 1978). In broad terms, three major self-interest motivations seem to drive international aid flows: (1) historical ties, (2) strategic behavior to encourage recipient countries to align their policies with donor foreign policy interests (support to the "war on terror," aid in exchange for votes in the UN Security Council), and (3) domestic political economy. In an influential paper, Alesina and Dollar (2000) looked at official development assistance (ODA) from different Organisation for Economic Co-operation and Development (OECD) countries and found that political and strategic variables were important determinants of aid, as is sharing a colonial past and having political alliances. They estimated that an inefficient, undemocratic, closed-economy country with colonial ties would actually receive more bilateral aid than a country that has similar poverty rates and better policies and institutions but does not share a colonial past with the donor.

Direct evidence of aid as an inducement to align the actions of recipients with donor objectives is well established. Studies that have explored the random rotation of countries to UN Security Council seats found a significant increase in ODA by donors like the United States when a recipient country has a seat (Kuziemko and Werker 2006). This effect is particularly pronounced during periods when key Security Council votes take place. Similar findings of vote inducement have been observed in the UN General Assembly (Dreher, Nunnenkamp, and Thiele 2008). Faye and Niehaus (2012) further documented how aid flows are timed so as to affect elections in recipient countries.

More recently, the war on terror has been shown to be an important driver of aid from OECD countries, in line with its increasing prominence in foreign policy agendas. Transnational terrorism poses a particular threat for the international community because, in principle, countries are sovereign and control their own counterterrorism policies. Third-party countries thus need to elicit cooperation from the host state to combat groups based there (Schultz 2010). Aid has also been used to incentivize a state's cooperation in combatting transnational terrorism, especially by the United States since the 9/11 attacks (Boutton and Carter 2014; Fleck and Kilby 2010). This antiterrorism agenda has been found to shape aid flows not only from the United States but also from other OECD countries (Bandyopadhyay and Vermann 2013; Dreher and Fuchs 2011).

The domestic political and economic interests of donors also influence the allocation of development aid. For instance, a vast literature shows how aid flows are linked to the trade interests of donor countries (Morrissey 1993; Osei, Morrissey, and Lloyd 2004), benefitting compatriot exporting firms. In the 1990s, trade-tied aid represented about half of total donor aid (Wagner 2003). Beyond the type of conditionality, OECD countries also allocate more aid funds to countries that rely more on imported goods in which the donor has a comparative production advantage (Younas 2008). More specific interests have also been shown to drive aid decisions, such as changes in food aid quantities driven by US government interests in stabilizing agricultural prices by exporting excess wheat production (Nunn and Qian 2014). Furthermore, the political ideology of politicians affects their preferences for the amount of aid flows (Milner and Tingley 2010) as well as the motivations and type of aid provided (Fleck and Kilby 2006).

Although analysis of the aid motives of individual countries suggests strategic drivers, these drivers are more prevalent in some countries than in others. For example, the Nordic countries and Switzerland allocate more aid on the basis of lower income and better institutions; France, Japan, and the United States emphasize strategic interests (Alesina and Dollar 2000; Berthélemy 2006). Also, the strategic nature of aid to influence votes in the UN General Assembly has been observed for the United States but not for other G-7 donors (Dreher, Nunnenkamp, and Thiele 2008).[2] Although scarcer, the evidence on the motivations of aid by non-OECD countries suggests that strategy also drives the allocation decision. There has been considerable debate about the motivations for Chinese aid, especially in Africa. Studies have found that Chinese aid is not conditioned on policy and institutional changes (such as democratic reforms) but rather on the use of Chinese goods and services (McCormick 2008) or in exchange for preferential energy deals. Thus, Chinese aid consists less of ODA and more of export credits, nonconcessional state loans, or aid linked to Chinese investment, thus promoting Chinese economic interests (Brautigam 2011; Tan-Mullins, Mohan, and Power 2010). Recent research has also demonstrated political motivations, with the birth regions of political leaders receiving greater foreign aid from China during periods when those leaders are in power; this effect is particularly pronounced when incumbents face upcoming elections and when electoral competitiveness is high (Dreher, Lang, and Richert 2019).

Revisiting the strategic motivations for foreign military interventions

As with foreign aid, foreign countries intervene in civil wars for diverse reasons that may not coincide with those of the side they are supporting and that may go beyond promoting the global public good of peace.[3] The political science literature has laid out such theories of the motivations for third-party interventions as preferences to reduce conflict and fatalities, including cessation of hostilities (Regan 2000); international strategic factors of potential intervening countries (Balch-Lindsay and Enterline 2000); or the desire to affect the balance of power between the two parties in conflict and thus influencing the dynamics and outcome of conflict (Gent 2008; Lemke and Regan 2004). Because military interventions are costly, countries choose them only when the risks or the opportunity costs of not intervening are even higher. In general, countries intervene to prevent the risk of conflict contagion; to preserve economic, social, and political interests and ties; or for domestic political economy reasons.

This report updates the analysis of foreign military interventions to cover the most recent period and study the prevalence of antiterrorism motivations. Although the changing nature of foreign interventions after the end of the Cold War has been recognized, most studies tend to include both pre– and post–Cold War periods in their analyses. The 9/11 attacks in the United States have further shifted the foreign policy agenda toward combatting global terrorism (Dreher and Fuchs 2011). In such circumstances, this chapter provides an original analysis of foreign interventions, restricting the period of analysis from the end of the Cold War (1991–2017). Looking at trends in foreign interventions starting at the end of the Cold War, one observes a significant increase in foreign military engagement after the 2001 terrorist attacks of 9/11. Given the preeminence of the war on terror agenda since the early 2000s, this report analyzes antiterrorist motivations as a driver of foreign interventions in civil wars over the last two decades, especially for the United States and its allies.

First, the chapter documents an increasing prevalence of foreign interventions in civil conflict. This analysis uses data on intrastate conflict from the Uppsala Conflict Data Program (UCDP) and follows the standard definition of civil war as episodes in which a country suffers more than 1,000 yearly battle-related deaths.[4] "Conflicts with foreign intervention" are counted as those where a foreign state enters the conflict with troops to actively support one side. According to this definition, 69 episodes of intrastate conflict have occurred since 1989; in 24 of these, at least one other country intervened.

The evolution of conflict over time shows that a large number of civil wars began in the late 1980s and early 1990s with the end of the Cold War and the breakdown of the Soviet Union. After a drop, since the mid-2000s the trend has again been upward (figure 3.2, panel a). Foreign countries intervened in about 55 percent of civil wars between 2004 and 2017, up considerably from less than 20 percent between 1989 and 2003. Since 2010, not only are intrastate conflicts more likely to be internationalized but more countries are also likely to be involved in foreign wars, from fewer than 10 in the early 1990s to more than 50 in every year since 2011 (figure 3.2, panel b).

Figure 3.2   Intrastate wars and the number of foreign countries intervening, 1990–2017

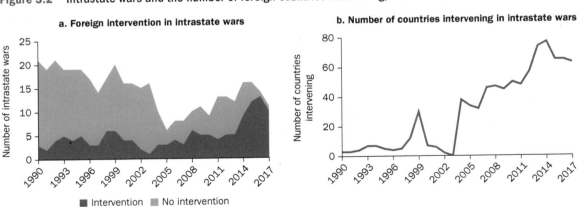

Source: Calculations based on Uppsala Conflict Data Program/Peace Research Institute Oslo Armed Conflict Dataset, version 19.1, https://www.prio .org/Data/Armed-Conflict/UCDP-PRIO/.

The increasing prevalence of foreign interventions is robust to controlling for differences in the likelihood of intervention in each country at war. This finding is important because the upward trend shown in figure 3.2 might be driven by unobserved conflict-specific variables. For example, a change in the profile of conflict over time could affect the incidence of foreign interventions. Figure 3.3 depicts the likelihood and its 95 percent confidence interval that, after accounting for country-specific fixed effects, a foreign intervention will occur for a country at war. Compared to the initial year of 1989, the likelihood of foreign interventions in intrastate conflicts has seen a progressive and significant upward trend.[5]

The increasing role of foreign interventions in intrastate conflict calls into question the traditional closed-economy approach to analyzing civil wars and highlights the need to understand what has been driving foreign interventions in recent years. Gleditsch (2007) was one of the first scholars to point out the transnational component of civil wars and how the traditional distinction between interstate and intrastate wars has become blurred. Countries can select whether to intervene directly or support a faction in a given country to promote their interests, what Salehyan (2010) calls the "delegation of war" to a rebel organization.

Figure 3.3   Likelihood of foreign interventions over time, 1990–2017

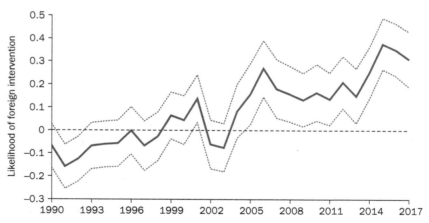

Source: Calculations based on Uppsala Conflict Data Program/Peace Research Institute Oslo Armed Conflict Dataset 2018, https://www.prio.org/Data/Armed-Conflict/UCDP-PRIO/.

Note: Coefficients and confidence interval of year fixed dummies in a regression of whether a country at war had a foreign intervention or not, controlling for country at war fixed effects (see annex 3A for methodological details).

A common reason for countries to intervene is to mitigate the risk of contagion from conflicts at their borders. Standard gravity equations of foreign interventions consistently show that contiguous countries are more likely to intervene in an intrastate conflict (see, for example, Kathman 2010; Martin, Mayer, and Thoenig 2008; Salehyan and Gleditsch 2006). The likelihood of intervention is higher when conflict spillovers could be derived from transnational ethnic ties (Buhaug and Gleditsch 2008) or because of possible destabilization due to the arrival of refugees that can affect ethnic balances and economic competition for resources (Salehyan and Gleditsch 2006).

Previous literature has found that economic, social, and political interests in the conflict-affected country are significant drivers of outside intervention. Countries are more likely to intervene militarily when they have bilateral trade and foreign direct investment flows with a country in conflict (Aidt and Albornoz 2011; Aydin 2008; Martin, Mayer, and Thoenig 2008), in countries with large oil reserves (Bove, Gleditsch, and Sekeris 2016), and to support coethnic groups that are active on one side of a civil war (Bove, Gleditsch, and Sekeris 2016; Buhaug and Gleditsch 2008; Gleditsch 2007; Kathman 2010). In terms of political ties, the evidence is mixed on whether a country is more likely to intervene when it has an alliance with a country at war (Koga 2011), and strategic geopolitical considerations beyond the country in question may also play a role (Kathman 2011). Finally, as with aid, domestic political reasons are a major driver of military interventions in foreign wars. Saideman (2001) has argued that domestic political competition leads certain countries to support specific groups in a foreign civil conflict, mainly groups that share ethnic ties with their domestic constituents. Albornoz and Hauk (2014) studied the role of domestic factors in the United States and estimated that the likelihood of intervention in a civil war around the world is significantly larger under a Republican administration and when the president's approval rates are lower.

To investigate the drivers of foreign interventions, the analysis for this chapter compiled bilateral data on conflict, geography, security, and historical, political, economic, and social ties. Following the analysis of Lemke and Regan (2004) often used in later studies, it uses panel data where every country can potentially intervene in any current civil war (all country pair combinations or dyads). Therefore, between 1989 and 2017, for every year in which one of the 69 coded civil wars continued, there is one observation for every third-party country (163 potential intervening countries). Of the total number of dyads (175,787) in the data, there are 1,033 foreign interventions.

Gravity-like specifications are estimated to understand the differing motivations countries have for intervening in other countries' domestic conflicts. Like previous studies, the analysis for this chapter includes (1) contiguity or neighbor effects, given the high likelihood of spillovers; (2) ethnic ties, measured by a dummy variable that takes the value of one if the two countries share a common ethnicity; (3) refugee flows (as a percent of the origin country's total population) as another measure of conflict spillovers; (4) bilateral trade (as a percent of GDP of both the country at war and the potentially intervening country) as a measure of economic interests and links between the two countries; (5) political alignments based on similarities in UN General Assembly voting; and (6) two alternative measures to capture the role of terrorism as a driver of foreign engagement in civil conflict. The first of the two measures relies on the central role of the United States in the war on terror, measured as the interaction of political alignment with the United States, based on UN voting, and whether the US State Department has designated any party in the conflict-affected country as a terrorist group.[6] The second measure aggregates the number of terrorist attacks in each potentially intervening country's territory or on its citizens by attackers from a country in conflict.[7] Furthermore, all regressions include other widely used control variables: log of distance between the two countries, common language, common religion, and common colonial ties.

The results of traditional determinants of foreign interventions for the post–Cold War period are generally in line with past studies. Figure 3.4 illustrates the regression results (details in annex 3A). Being a neighboring country and sharing ethnic ties increases the chances that one country will intervene in another country's civil war. The negative spillover of forced human displacement to third-party countries as a result of conflict is another key motivation for military engagement in that conflict. In particular, countries that receive refugees from the country in conflict are significantly more likely to intervene, and that probability increases with the size of the refugee inflow. This finding is consistent with Salehyan and Gleditsch (2006) and other studies that found refugees to be one channel through which conflict spreads—countries might want to intervene to prevent a further increase in the risk of contagion. When splitting the sample between contiguous and noncontiguous countries, the analysis finds that the impact of refugee flows on the likelihood of military interventions is focalized in countries that don't share a border (see models 10 and 11 in table 3A.2 in this chapter's annex), which suggests that countries

Figure 3.4   Drivers of foreign interventions in civil wars

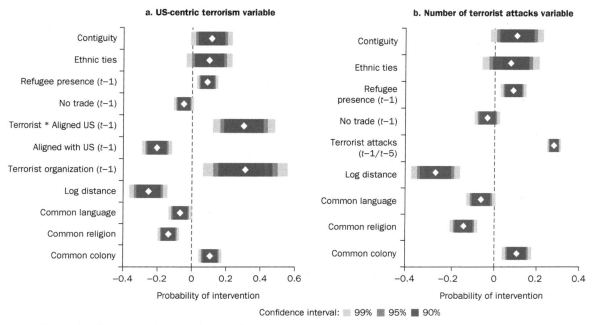

a. US-centric terrorism variable

b. Number of terrorist attacks variable

Probability of intervention

Probability of intervention

Confidence interval: 99% 95% 90%

Source: World Bank elaboration based on regression analysis.

Note: Results based on a linear probability model regression with fixed effects for country at war, potentially intervening country, and year. Following Martin, Mayer, and Thoenig (2008), the regression also includes dummies to control for temporal autocorrelation in wars. Coefficients represent the increase in the probability of intervention derived from a one standard deviation change in the explanatory variable. See annex 3A for data sources and empirical specifications.

that react to refugee flows might do so beyond the risks of conflict contagion. Bilateral trade ties are also associated, albeit weakly, with larger engagement in civil conflict. The positive association between trade ties and foreign interventions contrasts with the findings of Martin, Mayer, and Thoenig (2008), who saw a reduction in the likelihood of foreign interstate disputes. To reconcile those two findings, in the context of interstate conflict, bilateral trade can be damaged, whereas foreign interventions in intrastate conflicts mostly support the government in reducing instability and maintaining economic ties. As other studies have found, colonial ties, commonalities in language or religion, and distance are all significant predictors of the likelihood of foreign intervention.

Today, the "war on terror" seems to be one of the main triggers of foreign interventions in civil conflict. The analysis for this chapter finds robust evidence that, when one participant in a civil war has been classified by the US State Department as a terrorist organization, countries aligned with the United States are more likely to intervene for counterterrorism purposes. Similarly, the number of deaths related to terrorist attacks of individuals or organizations from a country at war during the previous five years significantly increases the likelihood that foreign countries will intervene in that civil conflict.[8] These results are robust to different specifications excluding one country at a time, specific regions like the Middle East and North Africa, or oil-exporting countries (see table 3A.2 in this chapter's annex for robustness checks), which shows the broad nature of this phenomenon.[9] The central role of counterterrorism on deciding to engage in foreign civil wars is observed only for nonneighbor countries, whereas neighbor countries are more driven by other motivations such as protecting coethnic groups or preventing contagion. As expected, when splitting the sample for the periods before and after 9/11, the counterterrorism motivation is significant for only the latter period. This change in the international relations agenda is in line with previous research that shows that foreign aid is increasingly focused on strategic counterterrorism partners (Fleck and Kilby 2010).

Effectiveness of third-party interventions

Estimating the effectiveness of third-party interventions is complicated by the patterns documented above, namely that such interventions do not occur in a vacuum and are dependent on a range of context characteristics. This complication can significantly affect the ability to infer the interventions' effectiveness. Beber (2012) documented that international mediation tends to occur in more-complex conflict situations. As a result, a correlation between mediation and civil conflict outcomes is likely to underestimate any impact. It might even be found that such interventions are associated with heightened violence that is due to the underlying features of the conflict rather than the intervention per se. If third-party interventions are believed to occur when peace is otherwise *less* likely, however, the estimates provided are more likely to be biased downward than upward. Fortna (2004) and Sambanis and Doyle (2007) showed that, on the basis of observable determinants of peacekeeping operations, the international community is more likely to intervene in the most complicated cases (such as inconclusive ends to a war or where there are no big government militaries) where peace agreements are more likely to derail into another war. Despite this potential bias, Gilligan and Sergenti (2008) still found that UN interventions are associated with longer-lasting peace but have no significant effects on the likelihood of reaching a peace agreement during a civil war.

Carnegie and Mikulaschek (forthcoming) use the quasi-random rotating membership of countries in the UN Security Council to show that states that wield more power send more peacekeepers to their preferred locations. The presence of these peacekeepers reduces civilian fatalities inflicted by rebels, but not those caused by governments. This finding corroborates earlier studies that also found UN peacekeeping missions to be associated with reduced conflict violence (Doyle and Sambanis 2000, 2006; Fortna 2004; Hultman, Kathman, and Shannon 2013, 2014; Ruggeri, Dorussen, and Gizelis 2017).

Despite those findings, the literature on foreign interventions in individual countries casts some doubt about whether the interventions reduce the duration of conflict. As for overall impact, studies have found that interventions by foreign countries are associated with longer and more lethal conflicts (Elbadawi and Sambanis 2000; Fearon 2008; Regan 2002; Sawyer, Cunningham, and Reed 2017; Wood, Kathman, and Gent 2012). Moreover, a war lasts longer when different countries intervene on opposite sides (Aydin and Regan 2012; Regan 2002). In only a few instances did studies find a shorter conflict, such as one-sided interventions by a country whose preferences are similar (Aydin and Regan 2012) or when foreign countries support the opposition group rather than the government (Collier, Hoeffler, and Soderbom 2004).

More recent data allow for evaluating whether these correlations persist in a post–Cold War world.[10] Like previous research, the current analysis finds that conflicts in the post–Cold War era last longer when third parties are involved. Cox hazard models of duration of war show that, for any given year, foreign interventions are associated with a 77 percent higher likelihood that the war will continue (figure 3.5, panel a).[11]

In other words, in 38 percent of civil wars without foreign intervention, conflict ends within a year, compared to only 4 percent when a third-party country has actively intervened. As with UN peacekeeping operations, however, other countries might intervene militarily in more protracted conflicts that, because of their very nature, would last longer independent of any foreign intervention. Panel b of figure 3.5 supports this conjecture: it shows the likelihood that a country will intervene in an internationalized intrastate conflict by year into the war, accounting for the number of continuing conflicts in each year; the upward trend suggests that foreign countries are more likely to intervene as the conflict becomes protracted.[12]

Figure 3.5 Probability that a war will continue and probability of foreign intervention, by length of war

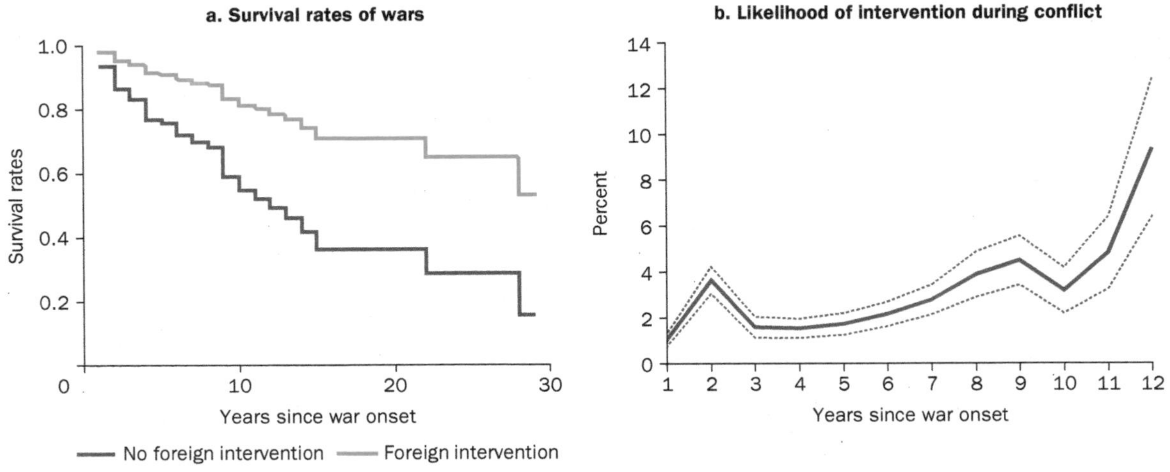

Source: World Bank elaboration based on Uppsala Conflict Data Program/Peace Research Institute Oslo Armed Conflict Dataset, version 19.1, https://www.prio.org/Data/Armed-Conflict/UCDP-PRIO/.

Limits to the effectiveness of third-party interventions

Although in theory a third party that is a benevolent and omniscient actor with perfect ability to commit to the terms of a contract can help to bring out peaceful resolutions, the institutions that have emerged as such third parties differ from the ideal. The ability of third parties to facilitate sustainable peace agreements hinges on some key assumptions: (1) that the actions and policies of both parties are fully observable by the third party, (2) that the third party can perfectly commit to following the terms of the contract, and (3) that there is only one such third party. Relaxing these hypotheses illuminates the limits of aid as a tool for addressing the cross-border spillovers of conflict, crime, and violence.

Third parties may have imperfect information about the environment and the actions of parties in conflict. In that case, the government might not have the same incentives to implement a given policy as the donor would wish, and the donor would not be able to incentivize its wishes. Devarajan and Swaroop (2000) thus advocate for a contract based on achieving goals rather than on financing projects. The problem is exacerbated by aid fungibility, in which funds earmarked for, say, security are substitutes for spending the government would have undertaken anyway, thus freeing up resources for other uses—including theft by corrupt bureaucrats and politicians. For instance, Khilji and Zampelli (1994) established empirically the fungibility of US military and nonmilitary aid.

Furthermore, dynamic effects in the relationship between a donor and a recipient country can complicate the design of appropriate incentive packages. The "ratchet effect" introduces a trade-off when setting incentive schemes for recipient countries.[13] Take, for instance, the issue of wildlife trafficking and animal conservation. From a static standpoint, the more endangered the species, the steeper the incentives need to be for a producing country to dedicate appropriate resources to combat illegal harvesting. Dynamically, however, success in reducing poaching leads to lower risk of extinction and correspondingly lower financial incentives. Thus, high performance today is punished by lower compensation tomorrow; symmetrically, low performance today is rewarded with larger compensation tomorrow. In this way, a static incentive scheme can have perverse dynamic effects.

Another constraint on the effectiveness of development or military assistance arises from adverse selection (Azam and Laffont 2003). To continue with the example of animal conservation, adverse selection stems from the donor's uncertainty about the policy priorities of the recipient government: although range states (states that are home to wildlife) might put a high value on the survival of their indigenous fauna and flora, they have strategic motivations to pretend to value it less in order to obtain more external financial incentives for animal conservation. In such an adverse selection setting, the process through which the recipient country can credibly signal its policy priorities might involve extended periods of time where it pretends not to care so as to build a reputation and extract larger concessions from donors (Kreps and Wilson 1982).

In situations involving such dynamic moral hazard or adverse selection, aid or any other foreign intervention might lead recipient countries to behave strategically in a way that worsens the situation more than no intervention. Whether the donor country can commit to withdrawal of aid is at the heart of what has been called the "Samaritan's dilemma" (Buchanan 1975). This principle highlights how public investment crowds out private investment. For instance, when a government provides relief after a natural disaster, it might induce citizens to decrease their take-up of disaster insurance, invest less in retrofitting their homes, and so on. It is easy to see how the concept applies to such aspects of society as intergenerational transfers, government social policy, charitable giving, and—relevant to this report—development or military assistance.

To solve the problem, Bruce and Waldman (1991) and Coate (1995) argued that in-kind transfers address the Samaritan's dilemma. In the context of international relations, the appropriate transfers would be nonfungible or marginal.

The presence of multiple third parties can also pose some challenges to preventing or reducing violence. If regional or global security is a public good, then each individual party has an incentive to contribute less than the optimal amount toward its production because of the well-known free-rider problem. Incentives of donors to dodge contributions to global public goods in order to achieve more donor-specific goals have also been found to increase with the number of donors (Knack and Rahman 2008). The generic result of such "common agency" models (see Bernheim and Whinston 1986; Grossman and Helpman 1994) is that individual third parties are worse off when they compete against one another. Bueno de Mesquita and Smith (2016) found that the Cold War brought a challenger to US hegemony, which resulted in the United States obtaining less in terms of security concessions while disbursing more aid. Conversely, if governments are less likely to invest in peacebuilding because of the presence of third-party contributions, then such underprovision due to free riding will have a lower social cost as governments reduce their shirking along this dimension (Torsvik 2005).

Multilateralism and the delegation of foreign interventions

The evidence so far seems to support a neorealist view of self-interested military interventions. As the emergence of multilateral organizations and global coalitions suggests, however, a neoliberal perspective on international relations acknowledges that countries are willing to delegate some decision-making power to a multilateral agency (Hawkins et al. 2006; Nielson and Tierney 2003). Delegation to a single multilateral third party is desirable when a group of individual self-interested parties is confronted by one or several of the issues discussed in the previous section. Several authors have analyzed this issue theoretically. For example, Milner and Tingley (2013) view country bilateral aid commitments as substitutes for each other; the aid commitments of a multilateral, such as the International Development Association replenishment rounds, are made complements in part thanks to the publicity around country pledges. Rodrik (1996) argues that the strength of multilateralism lies in its ability to turn donor competition into donor collaboration so as to ensure more-effective enforcement of agreements with recipient countries. Finally, Svensson (2000) discusses how delegation of aid to an institution may lead to a lower degree of the "Samaritan's dilemma" and thereby lead to gains in efficiency for both donors and recipients.

Does aid effectiveness depend on whether the aid flow is bilateral or multilateral? Such research is subject to numerous caveats. As noted, the delegation of aid to a multilateral agency to overcome collective bargaining failures makes multilateral and bilateral aid complements rather than substitutes. Thus, from a policy standpoint, whether one is preferable to the other is irrelevant. Empirically, too, aid flows might be driven by the geopolitical interests (or lack thereof) of donor countries, so that comparisons between the two are difficult to interpret causally: (1) the circumstances of the intervention differ depending on whether the third party is a country or a multilateral agency, and (2) the objectives of development assistance might also differ greatly. Nonetheless, establishing that the type of aid matters is an important first step to understanding what determines aid effectiveness in general.

Studies to date indicate that multilateral aid is likely to be more effective than bilateral aid. Aid from multilateral organizations has a larger focus on poor countries and is more need-based than aid from bilateral donors (Burnside and Dollar 2000; Frey and Schneider 1986; Neumayer 2003). Multilateral aid tends to favor good policies more than bilateral aid does (Burnside and Dollar 2000), and it also tends to follow better practices in being more transparent, specialized, or selective (Easterly and Pfutze 2008). In general, need-based aid has also been found to be more effective than politically motivated aid for economic growth, though the results are concentrated in countries where the macroeconomic outlook was weak to begin with (Dreher et al. 2013; Dreher, Lang, and Richert 2019; Kilby and Dreher 2010).

A similar empirical exercise can be undertaken for military interventions, with the same theoretical and empirical caveats. To date, however, little evidence has been provided to compare the efficiency of one form of military intervention with another.

Although the very existence of multilateral agencies is a clear sign that sovereign nations can set up institutions to promote global public goods, competition between countries has permeated international institutions.

For instance, Frey and Schneider (1986) looked at the World Bank's lending patterns and found that political as well as economic variables explained choices of which countries received loans. Similarly, Barro and Lee (2005) show how International Monetary Fund (IMF) loan allocations were shaped by the size of the recipient country's quota, the share of its nationals in the IMF professional staff, and the political and economic ties the country has with OECD countries. Using plausibly exogenous variations in the rotation of temporary members of the UN Security Council, several studies have shown preferential treatment to temporary members by such development organizations as the IMF (Dreher, Sturm, and Vreeland 2009a, 2015), the World Bank (Dreher, Sturm, and Vreeland 2009b; Kilby 2013), and the UN (Kuziemko and Werker 2006). Furthermore, Dreher, Lang, and Richert (2019) show that the joint influence of recipient countries and the countries of origin of the main contracting firms as International Finance Corporation stakeholders helps them access larger shares of the organization funds than purely needs-based considerations would justify. Although multilateral agencies can mitigate the free-riding problem, they are accountable to several countries with differing strategic objectives and differing political weight. How preferences of stakeholders are aggregated to form an agency's mandate will determine an agency's independence.

Concluding remarks and policy recommendations

This chapter has discussed the internationalization of conflict, crime, and violence on three dimensions and documented the transborder spillovers from domestic crime and conflict. The international trade in illicit drugs, wildlife products, and possibly small arms and human trafficking is expanding; instances of international terrorism have accelerated; and in recent years civil conflicts have become more common. These conflicts impose high costs on neighboring countries and beyond as countries become more economically interdependent, more refugees flee violence, and those refugees travel farther to seek safety. Conversely, every nation is influenced more by events and policies in other countries. Global commodity price shocks have been documented as shaping the dynamics of civil conflict; market regulation and demand in consumer countries influence crime in producing and transit countries.

The rising transnationality of conflict, crime, and violence means that domestic political stability and law enforcement capability have now become regional and global public goods. Furthermore, increased global integration makes some policies more susceptible to affect the incidence of conflict, crime, and violence. These two circumstances, regional or global public goods and "beggar-thy-neighbor" policies, create the scope for global governance institutions to play a role in the provision of global security.[14]

A plea for improving conflict, crime, and violence statistics for research and policy analyses

The analysis for this report took stock of an expanding literature on the macro- and microeconomic determinants of internal conflict, crime, and violence. It finds considerable evidence that transborder factors play a large role in shaping the opportunity costs as well as the returns from engaging in crime or conflict. The evidence base on other determinants such as state capacity or conflict contagion is a little more tenuous because these factors are difficult to measure.

One key driver behind the expansion of the knowledge base has been the increased availability of data on civil conflict, terrorism, and crime. The recent proliferation of disaggregated data on the incidence of transnational crimes, civil conflicts, and acts of terror has allowed researchers to undertake more-complex tests on their determinants as well as their impact on various aspects of human activity. The introduction of these new data has been partly the result of increased attention to the economic and social significance of these problems and partly due to the introduction of new technologies that have allowed their systematic collection.

For example, improvements in data on precise locations and attributes of instances of maritime piracy have resulted from the introduction of increased surveillance and geo-tracking of vessels, which has allowed for automatic and real-time identification of piracy attacks. This change has been instrumental in allowing for more complete coverage of attacks; however, gaps still exist within these data and need to be addressed. Although piracy along the Somali coast received great attention, providing impetus for the collecting of a comprehensive dataset on attacks in the region, a 2019 International Maritime Bureau report found that roughly 48 percent of piracy events within the Gulf of Guinea remain unreported (IMB 2019). Similarly, the quality of data on instances of human smuggling, trafficking of drugs, arms, and trade in illegal wildlife products—because of the illicit nature of these activities—is very limited and needs more precise attention.

Many of these data come from authorities interceding within these trafficking channels, making the data highly dependent on the relative efficacy of individual law enforcement agencies and variable over time. A greater focus on capacity building of law enforcement and custom agencies along with the standardization of data collected will greatly improve the quality of information available on the scale and prevalence of these transnational criminal markets.

The quality of data on armed conflicts has perhaps received the most focus, with the presence of multiple datasets at different levels of geographic and temporal aggregation. Gaps remain within these data, however, potentially biasing empirical exercises. As noted in box 1.1 in chapter 1, most of these data either come from military sources operating within fragile areas or are coded from media outlets (like newspapers). Although the former type of source is prone to underreporting events where the security organizations are not directly involved (for example in the targeting of civilians by nonstate actors), the latter suffers from a biased focus on incidents that take place in larger urban areas (as opposed to remote areas where events go unreported by media outlets). More attention is warranted in combining data on conflict events from multiple sources in order to develop a fuller picture. For terrorist attacks, the most widely used dataset has been the Global Terrorism Database (GTD), housed at the START Consortium at the University of Maryland. Since 2012, the US State Department has funded the work of the GTD after the National Counterterrorism Center (NCTC) discontinued its Worldwide Incidents Tracking System (WITS) database. More recently, the State Department's decision not to continue financing the GTD had brought the continued operation of the data project under question, but the Department of Defense Combating Terrorism Technical Support Office has appeased concerns by agreeing to continue funding of the data project. This inconsistency points to the precarious nature of financing of these global public goods that should be safeguarded.

Finally, theoretical and empirical studies of conflict seem to have been on two separate tracks. On the one hand, the contest success game described in this report has become the workhorse model to analyze strategic behavior in conflict. On the other hand, empirical analyses have primarily considered instances of violence and use fatality counts as the measure of conflict "intensity." For example, civil conflicts and wars are defined by a conflict casualty cutoff, yet contest success functions associate investments by each of the parties with a *probability* of winning and, in their current form, do not make any predictions when it comes to conflict violence or fatality counts. The link between theoretical predictions and empirical validations is thus still weak and deserves further exploration.

Upholding the "do-no-harm" principle in the provision of foreign assistance

The aid effectiveness literature has long identified economic or policy pitfalls of aid in that it might lead to "aid dependence" or that foreign aid flows may crowd out private or government investments. In the context of internal conflict, crime, and violence, the "do-no-harm" principle comprises several other dimensions.

The report makes a strong case for increased assistance to countries in their quest for political stability and crime eradication. The role of foreign assistance becomes starker when fragile countries face steeper fiscal constraints and thus puts the international community as lender of last resort. Nonetheless, this chapter has documented extensively the empirical evidence of potential negative impacts of aid on internal conflict and violence. When aid flows affect the returns to violence or have the potential to significantly strengthen state capacity, they can lead to an increase in violence as the parties reevaluate their strategies. Thus, in fragile settings, the question no longer is restricted to whether a development project will have a positive impact but also concerns whether it will further destabilize an already volatile situation. The complementarity between aid flows and security then becomes a critical element in donor or government engagement strategies, thus calling for more integration between the security and development sectors.

Furthermore, with countries increasingly exposed to the consequences of events occurring and policies adopted in foreign nations, the "do-no-harm" principle also applies across borders. When countries regulate a domestic market, that regulation has implications for countries upstream or downstream of such markets. Scholars and policy makers in animal conservation understand how consumer market regulation is critical to the fight against wildlife poaching in range states. When it comes to drugs, however, consumer market regulation is often linked to violence in producing and transit countries. Moreover, market forces imply that drug production eradication in one location may lead to the displacement of drug production to another location. Thus, the reality of transborder spillovers of market regulation should be met with increased policy coordination across countries, in either bilateral or multilateral forums, so that development policies in one country do not translate into heightened internal conflict, crime, and violence in another.

Strengthening partnerships and expanding the set of instruments for the provision of regional and global security

The provision of regional and global security requires coordination mechanisms to address the collective action problem inherent to the procurement of public goods. Alternatively, when policies adopted in one country have "beggar-thy-neighbor" effects—that is, they have the potential to affect the political stability or crime environment in another—coordination can create large efficiency gains. As discussed by Coase (1960), a collective resolution, also known as a Coasian solution, can be obtained if transaction costs are low enough. Because an increasingly integrated world implies greater needs for coordination across countries, the international community has a role to provide a forum and identify and create the instruments to address the aforementioned collective action problem. Recognizing that multilateral agencies are accountable to stakeholders with differing objectives and political weight, their mandate is constrained by how individual objectives are aggregated. Partnership then becomes critical when instruments of regional and global security span the humanitarian, development, and security sectors and involve finding a political resolution between warring parties.

ANNEX 3A   The determinants of foreign interventions in civil conflict

The analysis for this chapter uses data on intrastate conflicts from the UCDP for 1989–2017. Intrastate conflict is defined as a conflict between a government and a nongovernmental domestic party. The UCDP codes all third-party interventions when they enter a conflict with troops to actively support either the government or the opposition group regardless of the number of battle-related deaths inflicted or suffered. As is standard in the literature, the current analysis defines a country as being at war when the conflict results in at least 1,000 battle-related fatalities within a year. The duration of war is computed as all consecutive years with more than 1,000 deaths each. If deaths drop below 1,000 but surpass the 1,000-deaths-per-year threshold within three years, the war is considered to have continued.

As noted, the period of analysis is 1989–2017; most previous studies cover 1950–2000. Although many of those studies acknowledge that the nature of conflict changed after the Cold War, the period they cover means that they cannot shed much light on the more recent dynamics of internationalized civil conflict, especially since 9/11. That is the main reason why the sample in the current analysis is restricted to the years since the Cold War ended.

The analysis identified 69 civil wars from 1989 on; of those 69 civil wars, 24 had a foreign intervention and 45 did not. The extent of outside intervention varies widely, ranging from a single country intervening in 13 civil wars to 19 countries in 1999 in the Kosovo war, 38 countries in the mid-2000s civil war in Iraq, and 51 countries in the mid-2000s civil war in Afghanistan. Since 1989, 151 foreign countries have intervened in 24 civil wars.

Following up on the work of Lemke and Regan (2004) and subsequent studies, the current analysis used all country-pair combinations (dyads), assuming that every country could intervene in any civil war. Therefore, for every year between 1989 and 2017 in which one of the 69 coded civil wars was continuing, there is one observation for every potential intervening country (163). Of the total sample of 175,787 dyad-year observations, foreign intervention occurred in 1,033. The small share of foreign interventions is similar to the findings of Martin, Mayer, and Thoenig (2008), who define foreign engagement differently and study interstate rather than intrastate wars (in their study, 1,223 of 223,788 dyad-years involved conflict).

The current analysis combined the conflict data with data from the CEPII databases[15] (Gravity Geodist and Language), which provide matrixes of variables related to relations between any pair of countries (common border, common region, distance between the two countries, common language, common religion, common historical legal system, colony relationship, common colonizer [siblings], common currency, bilateral trade). *Contiguity* measures whether the third party and the country at war have a common border. *Colony* is a dummy variable taking value one for any pair ever in colonial relationship. *Sibling* is a dummy for country pairs with a common colonizer. *Common language* is a dummy that equals one if the same language is spoken by at least 9 percent of the population in both countries. *Common religion* is an index calculated by adding the products of the shares of Catholics, Protestants, and Muslims in each pair of countries and is bounded between zero and one (Disdier and Mayer 2007, based on La Porta et al. 1998). *Bilateral trade* is calculated as the arithmetic average of exports and imports between two countries as a percentage of their GDP. *Nobiltrade* is a dummy variable that takes the value one when the two countries do not trade between them—these are not missing values. One-year lagged trade from the onset of the civil war was used to mitigate endogeneity with the decision whether or not to intervene. Annual *bilateral refugee* flows were obtained from the UN High Commissioner for Refugees Population Statistics Database for 1950–2017.[16]

To measure political relations between two countries (*align UN voting*), the analysis obtained the correlation between how the two countries voted on resolutions in the UN General Assembly and used an index of political alliance compiled and constructed by Voeten, Strezhnev, and Bailey (2009) for the years 1946–2017.[17] Data on terrorist organizations are from the US State Department Bureau of Counterterrorism and Countering Violent Extremism. The first measure of counterterrorism motivation in foreign interventions is an interaction variable between (1) a dummy of whether any side in a country at war i in time t has been categorized as a terrorist organization by the US State Department; and (2) the level of political alliance of potential intervening country j with the US ($terrorism_{it} * align\ US_{jt})_{ijt}$. The assumption is that the closer a country j's alliance with the United States, the more likely it is that the country recognizes the US definition of terrorist groups and thus is more likely to have a similar counterterrorism motivation when intervening in a country where one such group is present. Note that data on UN voting alignment with the United States are far more complete than data on alignment for all bilateral pairs. Beyond this US-centric measure of counterterrorism, the analysis also uses a broader and more factual measure of terrorist attacks using the GTD and covering transnational and international terrorist incidents since 1970—a variable that is the number of killings in terrorist attacks in the years $t–1$ to $t–5$ perpetrated by an attacker from country i at war either in the territory of country j or on its citizens elsewhere.

The following gravity-like specification is estimated to understand what exactly motivates foreign countries to intervene in another country's domestic conflict (see table 3A.1). The literature review particularly analyzed the following determinants: (1) *contiguity*$_{ij}$, neighbor effects, given the higher likelihood of spillovers; (2) *ethnic ties*$_{ij}$, measured by a dummy variable that takes the value of one if the two countries share a common ethnicity; (3) the flow of *refugees*$_{ijt-1}$, another measure of spillover derived as $\left(\dfrac{refugees_{ijt-1}}{population_{jt-1}} \right)$; (4) *btrade*$_{ijt-1}$ as a measure of economic interests and

Table 3A.1 Drivers of foreign interventions in civil wars

Variables	Model (1)	Model (2)	Model (3)	Model (4)	Model (5)	Model (6)	Model (7)	Model (8)	Model (9)
Contiguity$_{ij}$	0.009***							0.005**	0.005*
	(0.003)							(0.0026)	(0.003)
Ethnic ties$_{ij}$		0.008***						0.004*	0.003
		(0.003)						(0.002)	(0.002)
Any refugees$_{ijt-1}$			0.003***					0.003***	0.003***
			(0.001)					(0.001)	(0.001)
Any trade$_{ijt-1}$				0.001**				0.0014**	0.001*
				(0.0005)				(0.0006)	(0.0006)
Align UN voting$_{ijt-1}$					−0.018***				
					(0.0054)				
Terror org$_{it-1}$*Align US$_{jt-1}$						0.028***		0.030***	
						(0.007)		(0.007)	
Terrorist$_{it-1}$						0.007***		0.009***	
						(0.002)		(0.002)	
Align US$_{jt-1}$						−0.018***		−0.024***	
						(0.003)		(0.004)	
Terrorist attacks$_{ijt-1/t-5}$							0.032***		0.031***
							(0.001)		(0.001)
Log distance$_{ij}$	−0.004***	−0.005***	−0.005***	−0.006***	−0.005***	−0.005***	−0.006***	−0.003***	−0.004***
	(0.0001)	(0.001)	(0.001)	(0.001)	(0.001)	(0.001)	(0.001)	(0.001)	(0.001)
Common language$_{ij}$	−0.001	−0.002**	−0.002**	−0.001	0.0004	−0.001	−0.001	−0.002***	−0.002***
	(0.001)	(0.001)	(0.001)	(0.001)	(0.001)	(0.001)	(0.001)	(0.001)	(0.001)
Common religion$_{ij}$	−0.005***	−0.006***	−0.004***	−0.005***	−0.005***	−0.004***	−0.005***	−0.005***	−0.005***
	(0.001)	(0.001)	(0.001)	(0.001)	(0.001)	(0.001)	(0.001)	(0.001)	(0.001)
Common colony$_{ij}$	0.004***	0.004***	0.004***	0.003***	0.003***	0.003***	0.004***	0.004***	0.004***
	(0.001)	(0.001)	(0.001)	(0.001)	(0.001)	(0.001)	(0.001)	(0.001)	(0.001)
Constant	0.052***	0.056***	0.054***	0.063***	0.074***	0.049***	0.059***	0.030***	0.046***
	(0.006)	(0.006)	(0.006)	(0.007)	(0.010)	(0.007)	(0.006)	(0.005)	(0.005)
Observations	62,465	62,302	58,281	62,465	48,787	62,465	59,567	58,120	55,222
R-squared	0.040	0.040	0.052	0.004	0.051	0.042	0.042	0.056	0.055
Year FE	Yes	Yes	Yes	Yes	Yes	Yes	Yes	Yes	Yes
Country *i* FE	Yes	Yes	Yes	Yes	Yes	Yes	Yes	Yes	Yes
Country *j* FE	Yes	Yes	Yes	Yes	Yes	Yes	Yes	Yes	Yes
War lags	Yes	Yes	Yes	Yes	Yes	Yes	Yes	Yes	Yes
Estimation method	FE LPM	FE LPM	FE LPM	FE LPM	FE LPM	FE LPM	FE LPM	FE LPM	FE LPM

Source: World Bank elaboration.
Note: Robust standard errors in parentheses. FE = fixed effect; LPM = linear probability model.
*** $p < 0.01$, ** $p < 0.05$, * $p < 0.1$.

links derived by $\left(\dfrac{trade_{ijt-1}}{GDP_{ijt-1}}\right)$; (5) political alignments in UN General Assembly voting (*align UN voting$_{ijt-1}$*); and, finally, (6) a measure of counterterrorism policy (*terror$_{ijt-1}$*), which is either the number of killings in terrorist attacks perpetrated by attackers from country i at war in territory of country j or on its citizens during the period $t-1$ to $t-5$ (*terrorist_ attacks$_{ijt-1/t-5}$*), or the interaction between whether any party in the civil conflict is recognized by the United States as a terrorist group and how aligned a country j may be with the United States (*terror$_{it-1}$ * align US$_{jt-1}$*). The regression equation is

$$
\begin{aligned}
intervention_{ijt} = &\; \alpha_1 \, contiguity_{ij} + \alpha_2 \, ethnic_{ij} + \alpha_3 \, refugees_{ijt-1} + \alpha_4 \, btrade_{ijt-1} \\
&+ \alpha_5 \, align \; UN \; voting_{ijt-1} + \alpha_6 \, terror_{ijt-1} + \alpha_7 \ln(distance_{ij}) \\
&+ \alpha_8 \, common\_language_{ij} + \alpha_9 \, common\_colony_{ij} \\
&+ \alpha_{10} \, common\_religion_{ij} + \delta_i + \delta_j + \delta_t + \varepsilon_{ijt}, \qquad (3A.1)
\end{aligned}
$$

where i is the country at war, j the potentially intervening country, and t time. The dependent variable, *intervention$_{ijt}$*, is a dummy variable taking the value of one for every year t that country j intervened in the country i civil war. In order to avoid endogeneity and autocorrelation, all observations are eliminated when a country j intervenes in conflict in country i if it had already intervened in the periods $t-1$ to $t-3$. The variable *refugees$_{ijt-1}$* is alternatively expressed as a dummy variable when there are no refugee flows from country i to country j, or the logarithm of the number of refugees from country i to country j, a share of country j's population. Similarly, the variable *btrade$_{ijt-1}$* is alternatively expressed as a dummy variable when there are no trade flows from country i to country j, or the logarithm of the average trade flows between country i to country j, a share of their GDPs.

Because the error term is likely to exhibit correlation patterns for a given country pair, the standard errors are first clustered at the dyadic pair level. Second, control variables typically used in the literature are added (*distance$_{ij}$, common_language$_{ij}$, common_colony$_{ij}$, common_religion$_{ij}$*) that can affect both the main explanatory variables and the probability of intervening in civil conflicts. Third-party country i, country j, and time fixed effects are added in a standard linear fixed effect specification to control for the potential trends over time and for specific country characteristics. The temporal autocorrelation in wars are controlled for by including 20 dummies equal to one when the country j intervened in country i in

$t-1$, $t-2$, ... $t-20$. As Martin, Mayer, and Thoenig (2008) argue, it is necessary to control for that because the effect of interventions on the dependent variables can be lasting. In the final specification all the drivers are added together and a series of robustness checks are provided.

Attempts to address some of the endogeneity issues include controlling for various codrivers of conflict; lagging endogenous variables to conflict (such as bilateral trade, refugee flows, political alignment and terrorist attacks); and including country-pair fixed effects and time effects. The results are robust to different specification strategies.

Results of the traditional determinants are in line with past literature. Being a neighbor country and sharing ethnic ties increase the chances of intervening in the other country's civil war (models 1 and 2). In both cases, the magnitudes are similar, about 1 percentage point. These magnitudes are large compared to the average probability of a foreign intervention (0.6 percent). When both variables are included in the same regression they lose some statistical and economic significance. In spite of the links between the two variables (neighboring countries are more likely to have common ethnic ties), being a neighbor is still significant after controlling for ethnic ties, which suggests other factors at play beyond ethnicity, such as the risks of spillovers, in explaining the higher likelihood that neighbors will intervene.

Moreover, the influx of refugees one year before the war period also raises the likelihood that a foreign country will intervene. Model 3 shows that, for 22 percent of countries that had refugees from the country at war before the conflict began, the probability of intervention increases by 0.3 percentage point. The findings are similar when including the log of refugees for the subsample of pair countries with at least one refugee. The more refugees it receives from the country in conflict, the more likely a country is to intervene.

Bilateral trade ties are also weakly associated with an increase in the likelihood of a country's decision to engage in foreign civil conflict. The analysis uses two measures of bilateral trade: (1) one dummy variable with value one when a pair of countries trades (67 percent of cases) and (2) the log of bilateral trade as a share of both countries' GDP when they have some trade one year before the war begins. Both variables are only weakly significant but maintain their significance in the final specification when all other explanatory variables are included (model 8).

Political alignment reduces the chances of foreign interventions. Model 5 shows that the more politically aligned a country is with the country at war (the higher the ratio of voting alike in the UN General Assembly), the less likely it is to engage in the war. This result is robust. when including all other covariates. Because the missing values on political alignment for all bilateral pairs reduce the sample significantly, this variable is not included in the final specifications (models 8 and 9).

Finally, countering terrorism is found to be a strong factor when intervention in foreign conflicts is being considered (models 6 and 8). Wars where the United States has categorized one of the sides as a terrorist group have a higher likelihood of outside interventions, especially by countries more politically aligned with the United States. In the same vein, countries that suffered a terrorist attack in the last five years from individuals or organizations based in the country in conflict are significantly more likely to intervene than those that didn't suffer any terrorist attack, and that likelihood increases the greater the number of victims in the attack (models 7 and 9). This prevalence of the war on terror in the international relations agenda supports previous studies demonstrating that US foreign aid is increasingly directed to strategic counterterrorism partners (Fleck and Kilby 2010).

Following Kathman (2010), models 10 and 11 in table 3A.2 split the sample between contiguous and noncontiguous countries because they have different motivations to intervene. Interestingly, contiguous countries seem mostly to intervene when they have ethnic ties with the country at war. Also, the negative association between political alignment and foreign intervention is driven by neighboring countries; nonneighboring countries seem to be motivated more by refugee spillovers, economic interests (trade), and counterterrorist concerns. In several instances, criticisms have been raised about a hidden agenda behind the war on terror based on economic interests to exploit oil in war-torn countries. To rule out the oil mechanism, model 12 restricts the sample to civil wars in countries that are not among the 30 main oil-exporting economies. Excluding these economies, results remain robust, showing a strong positive correlation between the war on terror variable and the decision to intervene in foreign civil wars. Finally, models 13–16 divide the sample between the periods before and after 9/11 for the two different measures of terrorism. In both cases, the counterterrorism motivation is significant only for the more recent period after 2001, which suggests a breaking point in the foreign policy arena after 9/11 with the rise of the counterterrorism agenda.

Table 3A.2 Results by contiguity and post-9/11 occurrence

Variables	Model (10) Intervene (contiguous)	Model (11) Intervene (noncontiguous)	Model (12) Intervene (non-oil)	Model (13) Intervene (post-9/11)	Model (14) Intervene (pre-9/11)	Model (15) Intervene (post-9/11)	Model (16) Intervene (pre-9/11)
$Contiguity_{ij}$			0.001	0.007	0.003	0.006	0.003
			(0.003)	(0.005)	(0.003)	(0.005)	(0.003)
$Ethnic\ ties_{ij}$	0.030**	0.001	0.013***	0.003	0.007*	0.003	0.004
	(0.015)	(0.003)	(0.005)	(0.004)	(0.004)	(0.004)	(0.004)
$Any\ refugees_{ijt-1}$	0.003	0.003***	0.003***	0.001	0.003***	0.002	0.003***
	(0.010)	(0.001)	(0.001)	(0.001)	(0.001)	(0.001)	(0.001)
$Any\ trade_{ijt-1}$	0.011	0.001***	0.000	0.006***	−0.002***	0.005***	−0.002***
	(0.015)	(0.0005)	(0.001)	(0.001)	(0.001)	(0.001)	(0.0005)
$Terror\ org{*}Align\ US_{ijt-1}$	0.120	0.031***	0.025***	0.061***	0.001		
	(0.196)	(0.007)	(0.008)	(0.013)	(0.003)		
$Terrorist_{it-1}$	0.065*	0.009***	0.002	0.013***	−0.000		
	(0.039)	(0.002)	(0.002)	(0.004)	(0.001)		
$Align\ with\ US_{jt-1}$	−0.012	−0.025***	−0.023***	−0.042***	−0.017***		
	(0.050)	(0.004)	(0.005)	(0.007)	(0.005)		
$Terrorist\ attacks_{ijt-1/t-5}$						0.029***	−0.003
						(0.001)	(0.001)
$Log\ distance_{ij}$	0.001	−0.003***	−0.004***	−0.005***	−0.003***	−0.005***	−0.003***
	(0.022)	(0.0005)	(0.001)	(0.001)	(0.001)	(0.001)	(0.0007)
$Common\ language_{ij}$	−0.033**	−0.001**	−0.002***	0.004**	−0.002**	0.004**	−0.001**
	(0.016)	(0.0005)	(0.0005)	(0.002)	(0.001)	(0.002)	(0.0007)
$Common\ religion_{ij}$	0.023	−0.004***	−0.004***	−0.009***	−0.002**	−0.011***	−0.001*
	(0.030)	(0.001)	(0.001)	(0.002)	(0.001)	(0.002)	(0.0007)
$Common\ colony_{ij}$	0.048*	0.003***	0.004***	0.008***	0.002**	0.007***	0.003**
	(0.025)	(0.001)	(0.001)	(0.002)	(0.001)	(0.002)	(0.001)
Constant	−0.023	0.029***	0.043***	0.048***	0.026***	0.074***	0.023***
	(0.181)	(0.005)	(0.007)	(0.010)	(0.006)	(0.011)	(0.006)
Observations	1,743	56,337	44,319	22,774	35,346	22,774	32,448
R-squared	0.254	0.062	0.050	0.069	0.074	0.066	0.080
Year FE	Yes	Yes	Yes	Yes	Yes	Yes	Yes
Country i FE	Yes	Yes	Yes	Yes	Yes	Yes	Yes
Country j FE	Yes	Yes	Yes	Yes	Yes	Yes	Yes
War lags	Yes	Yes	Yes	Yes	Yes	Yes	Yes
Estimation method	FE LPM	FE LPM	FE LPM	FE LPM	FE LPM	FE LPM	FE LPM

Source: World Bank elaboration.

Note: Robust standard errors in parentheses. FE = fixed effect; LPM = linear probability model.

*** $p < 0.01$, ** $p < 0.05$, * $p < 0.1$.

Notes

1. A Pigouvian subsidy is a subsidy to an activity that generates positive benefits to society at large.
2. The G-7, or Group of Seven countries, consists of Canada, France, Germany, Italy, Japan, the United Kingdom, and the United States.
3. Similarly, third parties are more likely to offer to mediate conflicts when they have historical ties with the country in conflict or when they have vested interests (Greig and Regan 2008).
4. Annex 3A details the data and methodology.
5. The results are robust to excluding any individual civil war from the sample, and therefore are not driven by any particular episode of conflict.
6. Political alignment with the United States (align_with_US$_{jt}$) is a discrete variable that captures the percentage of times that a country agrees with the United States in UN General Assembly resolutions, ranging from zero to one (full agreement); being listed by the United States as a terrorist organization is a dummy variable taking value one if the State Department classified any of the parties involved in the conflict as a terrorist organization. The variables are lagged one period to mitigate endogeneity problems. The created interaction variable is then time, country$_i$ and country$_j$ variant: $(terrorism_{it-1} *align\_with\_US_{jt-1})_{ijt-1}$. The assumption is that the closer a country j is allied with the United States, the more likely it is that it recognizes the US definition of terrorist groups and thus is more likely to have a similar counterterrorism motivation when intervening in a country where one such group is present.
7. In particular, the variable is the sum of killings in terrorist attacks in the years $t-1$ to $t-5$ perpetrated by an attacker from country j at war either in territory of country j or on its citizens elsewhere (see annex 3A for more details and data sources).
8. Robustness checks dropping one country in conflict at a time show that these results are not driven by any single country. Results do not significantly change either when restricting the sample to non-oil-exporting countries, so oil is not a confounding factor that drives the results on the impact of terrorism variables on the likelihood of intervention.
9. Only when both the Afghanistan and Iraq wars are excluded from the sample does the impact of terrorism become insignificant, although this result is driven by the reduced sample size of foreign interventions in other countries.
10. To evaluate the duration of civil conflict, analysis follows standard methodology by which a country is considered at war when annual battle-related deaths are more than 1,000. If there is a drop below 1,000 for two years or less, the war is considered to have continued. With this definition, between 1989 and 2017 the average duration of a civil war was 5.75 years, though the average conceals a large variation, with conflicts ranging from 1 to 29 years.
11. This correlation is statistically significant after controlling for year fixed effects, with a p-value of 0.019.
12. These results exclude both the Afghanistan and Iraq wars, which have much larger numbers of foreign interventions so that those two conflicts do not drive all the results. When both are included, the main message of lagging foreign intervention once the conflict is ongoing does not change.

13. The ratchet effect was first studied by Berliner (1957) and later analyzed by Weitzman (1980) and many others (see discussion in Laffont and Tirole 1993) in the context of incentive contracts within a business. Bapat (2011) then applied it to the analysis of security and military aid.
14. Rodrik (2019) discusses the place for global governance in an increasingly integrated world.
15. For more information on CEPII (Centre d'Etudes Prospectives et d'Informations Internationales) and its databases, see http://www.cepii.fr /CEPII/en/welcome.asp.
16. For more information, see http://popstats.unhcr.org/en/overview.
17. Their dataset, derived from the correlation between how two countries voted, was first published in 2009 but has since been extended to 2017.

References

Aidt, T., and F. Albornoz. 2011. "Political Regimes and Foreign Intervention." *Journal of Development Economics* 94 (2): 192–201.

Albornoz, F., and E. Hauk. 2014. "Civil War and US Foreign Influence." *Journal of Development Economics* 110: 64–78.

Alesina, A., and D. Dollar. 2000. "Who Gives Foreign Aid to Whom and Why?" *Journal of Economic Growth* 5 (1): 33–63.

Aydin, A. 2008. "Choosing Sides: Economic Interdependence and Interstate Disputes." *Journal of Politics* 70 (4): 1098–108.

Aydin, A., and P. M. Regan. 2012. "Networks of Third-Party Interveners and Civil War Duration." *European Journal of International Relations* 18 (3): 573–97.

Azam, J.-P., and J. J. Laffont. 2003. "Contracting for Aid." *Journal of Development Economics* 70 (1): 25–58.

Balch-Lindsay, D., and A. Enterline. 2000. "Killing Time: The World Politics of Civil War Duration, 1820–1992." *International Studies Quarterly* 44 (4): 615–42.

Bandyopadhyay, S., and E. K. Vermann. 2013. "Donor Motives for Foreign Aid." *Federal Reserve Bank of St. Louis Review* 95 (4): 327–36.

Bapat, N. A. 2011. "Transnational Terrorism, US Military Aid, and the Incentive to Misrepresent." *Journal of Peace Research* 48 (3): 303–18.

Barro, R. J., and J. W. Lee. 2005. "IMF Programs: Who Is Chosen and What Are the Effects?" *Journal of Monetary Economics* 52 (7): 1245–69.

Beardsley, K., D. Cunningham, and P. White. 2017. "Resolving Civil Wars before They Start: The UN Security Council and Conflict Prevention in Self-Determination Disputes." *British Journal of Political Science* 47 (3): 675–97.

Beber, B. 2012. "International Mediation, Selection Effects, and the Question of Bias." *Conflict Management and Peace Science* 29 (4): 397–424.

Bergström, T., L. Blume, and H. Varian. 1986. "On the Private Provision of Public Goods." *Journal of Public Economics* 29 (1): 25–49.

Berliner, J. S. 1957. *Factory and Manager in the Soviet Union*. Cambridge, MA: Harvard University Press.

Bernheim, B. D., and M. D. Whinston. 1986. "Common Agency." *Econometrica: Journal of the Econometric Society* 54 (4): 923–42.

Berthélemy, J. C. 2006. "Bilateral Donors' Interest vs. Recipients' Development Motives in Aid Allocation: Do All Donors Behave the Same?" *Review of Development Economics* 10 (2): 179–94.

Boutton, A., and D. B. Carter. 2014. "Fair-Weather Allies? Terrorism and the Allocation of US Foreign Aid." *Journal of Conflict Resolution* 58 (7): 1144–73.

Bove, V., K. S. Gleditsch, and P. G. Sekeris. 2016. "Oil above Water: Economic Interdependence and Third-Party Intervention." *Journal of Conflict Resolution* 60 (7): 1251–77.

Brautigam, D. 2011. "Aid 'with Chinese Characteristics': Chinese Foreign Aid and Development Finance Meet the OECD-DAC Aid Regime." *Journal of International Development* 23 (5): 752–64.

Brooks, S., and W. Wohlforth. 2008. *World Out of Balance: International Relations and the Challenge of American Primacy.* Princeton, NJ: Princeton University Press.

Bruce, N., and M. Waldman. 1991. "Transfers in Kind: Why They Can Be Efficient and Nonpaternalistic." *American Economic Review* 81 (5): 1345–51.

Buchanan, J. M. 1975. "The Samaritan's Dilemma." In *Altruism, Morality, and Economic Theory*, edited by Edmund S. Phelps, 71–85. New York: Russell Sage Foundation.

Bueno de Mesquita, B., and A. Smith. 2016. "Competition and Collaboration in Aid-for-Policy Deals." *International Studies Quarterly* 60 (3): 413–26.

Buhaug, H., and K. S. Gleditsch. 2008. "Contagion or Confusion? Why Conflicts Cluster in Space." *International Studies Quarterly* 52 (2): 215–33.

Burnside, C., and D. Dollar. 2000. "Aid, Policies, and Growth." *American Economic Review* 90 (34): 847–68.

Carnegie, A., and C. Mikulaschek. Forthcoming. "The Promise of Peacekeeping: Protecting Civilians in Civil War." *International Organization.*

Coase, R. H. 1960. "The Problem of Social Cost." *Journal of Law and Economics* 3: 1–44.

Coate, S. 1995. "Altruism, the Samaritan's Dilemma, and Government Transfer Policy." *American Economic Review* 85 (1): 46–57.

Collier, P., A. Hoeffler, and M. Soderbom. 2004. "On the Duration of Civil War." *Journal of Peace Research* 41 (3): 253–73.

Devarajan, S., and V. Swaroop. 2000. "The Implications of Foreign Aid Fungibility for Development Assistance." In *The World Bank: Structure and Policies*, edited by C. L. Gilbert and D. Vines, 196–209. New York: Cambridge University Press.

Disdier, A.-C., and T. Mayer. 2007. "Je t'aime, moi non plus: Bilateral Opinions and International Trade." *European Journal of Political Economy* 23 (4): 1140–59.

Doyle, M., and N. Sambanis. 2000. "International Peacebuilding: A Theoretical and Quantitative Analysis." *American Political Science Review* 94 (4): 779–801.

———. 2006. *Making War and Building Peace: United Nations Peace Operations.* Princeton, NJ: Princeton University Press.

Dreher, A., and A. Fuchs. 2011. "Does Terror Increase Aid?" *Public Choice* 149 (3–4): 337–63.

Dreher, A., S. Klasen, J. R. Vreeland, and E. Werker. 2013. "The Costs of Favoritism: Is Politically Driven Aid Less Effective?" *Economic Development and Cultural Change* 62 (1): 157–91.

Dreher, A., V. F. Lang, and K. Richert. 2019. "The Political Economy of International Finance Corporation Lending." *Journal of Development Economics* 140: 242–54.

Dreher, A., P. Nunnenkamp, and R. Thiele. 2008. "Does US Aid Buy UN General Assembly Votes? A Disaggregated Analysis." *Public Choice* 136 (1–2): 139–64.

Dreher, A., J. E. Sturm, and J. R. Vreeland. 2009a. "Global Horse Trading: IMF Loans for Votes in the United Nations Security Council." *European Economic Review* 53 (7): 742–57.

———. 2009b. "Development Aid and International Politics: Does Membership on the UN Security Council Influence World Bank Decisions?" *Journal of Development Economics* 88 (1): 1–18.

———. 2015. "Politics and IMF Conditionality." *Journal of Conflict Resolution* 59 (1): 120–48.

Easterly, W., and T. Pfutze. 2008. "Where Does the Money Go? Best and Worst Practices in Foreign Aid." *Journal of Economic Perspectives* 22 (2): 29–52.

Elbadawi, I. A., and N. Sambanis. 2000. "External Interventions and the Duration of Civil Wars." Policy Research Working Paper 2433, World Bank, Washington, DC.

Faye, M., and P. Niehaus. 2012. "Political Aid Cycles." *American Economic Review* 102 (7): 3516–30.

Fearon, J. D. 2008. "Economic Development, Insurgency and Civil War." In *Institutions and Economic Performance*, edited by Elhanan Helpman, 292–328. Cambridge, MA: Harvard University Press.

Fleck, R. K., and C. Kilby. 2006. "How Do Political Changes Influence US Bilateral Aid Allocations? Evidence from Panel Data." *Review of Development Economics* 10 (2): 210–23.

———. 2010. "Changing Aid Regimes? US Foreign Aid from the Cold War to the War on Terror." *Journal of Development Economics* 91 (2): 185–97.

Fortna, V. P. 2004. "Does Peacekeeping Keep Peace? International Intervention and the Duration of Peace after Civil War." *International Studies Quarterly* 48 (2): 269–92.

Frey, B. S., and F. Schneider. 1986. "Competing Models of International Lending Activity." *Journal of Development Economics* 20 (2): 225–45.

Fudenberg, D., and J. Tirole. 1991. *Game Theory*. Cambridge, MA: MIT Press.

Gent, S. E. 2008. "Going in When It Counts: Military Intervention and the Outcome of Civil Conflicts." *International Studies Quarterly* 52: 713–35.

Gilligan, M. J., and E. J. Sergenti. 2008. "Do UN Interventions Cause Peace? Using Matching to Improve Causal Inference." *Quarterly Journal of Political Science* 3 (2): 89–122.

Gleditsch, K. S. 2007. "Transnational Dimensions of Civil War." *Journal of Peace Research* 44 (3): 293–309.

Greig, M. J., and P. M. Regan. 2008. "When Do They Say Yes? An Analysis of the Willingness to Offer and Accept Mediation in Civil Wars." *International Studies Quarterly* 52 (4): 759–81.

Grossman, G., and E. Helpman. 1994. "Protection for Sale." *American Economic Review* 84 (4): 833–50.

Hawkins, D. G., D. A. Lake, D. L. Nielson, and M. Tierney. 2006. *Delegation and Agency in International Organizations.* Cambridge, UK: Cambridge University Press.

Hultman, L., J. Kathman, and M. Shannon. 2013. "United Nations Peacekeeping and Civilian Protection in Civil War." *American Journal of Political Science* 57 (4): 875–91.

———. 2014. "Beyond Keeping Peace: United Nations Effectiveness in the Midst of Fighting." *American Political Science Review* 108 (4): 737–53.

IMB (International Maritime Bureau). 2019. "Piracy and Armed Robbery against Ships: Annual Report." International Chamber of Commerce: Commercial Crime Services, London.

Karreth, J., and J. Tir. 2013. "International Institutions and Civil War Prevention." *Journal of Politics* 75 (1): 96–109.

Kathman, J. D. 2010. "Civil War Contagion and Neighboring Interventions." *International Studies Quarterly* 54 (4): 989–1012.

———. 2011. "Civil War Diffusion and Regional Motivations for Intervention." *Journal of Conflict Resolution* 55 (6): 847–76.

Khilji, N. M., and E. M. Zampelli. 1994. "The Fungibility of US Military and Non-military Assistance and the Impacts on Expenditures of Major Aid Recipients." *Journal of Development Economics* 43 (2): 345–62.

Kilby, C. 2013. "The Political Economy of Project Preparation: An Empirical Analysis of World Bank Projects." *Journal of Development Economics* 105 (C): 211–25.

Kilby, C., and A. Dreher. 2010. "The Impact of Aid on Growth Revisited: Do Donor Motives Matter?" *Economics Letters* 107 (3): 338–40.

Knack, S., and A. Rahman. 2008. "Donor Fragmentation." In *Reinventing Foreign Aid*, edited by W. Easterly, 333–48. Cambridge, MA: MIT Press.

Koga, J. 2011. "Where Do Third Parties Intervene? Third Parties, Domestic Institutions and Military Interventions in Civil Conflicts." *International Studies Quarterly* 55 (4): 1143–66.

Kreps, D. M., and R. Wilson. 1982. "Reputation and Imperfect Information." *Journal of Economic Theory* 27 (2): 253–79.

Kuziemko, I., and E. Werker. 2006. "How Much Is a Seat on the Security Council Worth? Foreign Aid and Bribery at the United Nations." *Journal of Political Economy* 114 (5): 905–30.

Laffont, J. J., and J. Tirole. 1993. *A Theory of Incentives in Procurement and Regulation.* Cambridge, MA: MIT Press.

La Porta, R., F. Lopez-de-Silanes, A. Shleifer, and R. W. Vishny. 1998. "Law and Finance." *Journal of Political Economy* 106 (6): 1113–55.

Lemke, D., and P. M. Regan. 2004. "Interventions as Influence." In *The Scourge of War: New Extensions on an Old Problem*, edited by Paul Diehl, 145–68. Ann Arbor: University of Michigan Press.

Martin, P., T. Mayer, and M. Thoenig. 2008. "Make Trade Not War?" *Review of Economic Studies* 75 (3): 865–900.

McCormick, D. 2008. "China and India as Africa's New Donors: The Impact of Aid on Development." *Review of African Political Economy* 35 (115): 73–92.

McKinlay, R. D. 2006. "The German Aid Relationship: A Test of the Recipient Need and the Donor Interest Models of the Distribution of German Bilateral Aid, 1961–70." *European Journal of Political Research* 6 (3): 235–57.

McKinlay, R. D., and R. Little. 1977. "A Foreign Policy Model of US Bilateral Aid Allocation." *World Politics* 30 (1): 58–86.

———. 1978. "The French Aid Relationship: A Foreign Policy Model of the Distribution of French Bilateral Aid, 1964–70." *Development and Change* 9 (3): 459–78.

Milner, H. V., and D. H. Tingley. 2010. "The Political Economy of US Foreign Aid: American Legislators and the Domestic Politics of Aid." *Economics and Politics* 22 (2): 200–32.

———. 2013. "The Choice for Multilateralism: Foreign Aid and American Foreign Policy." *Review of International Organizations* 8 (3): 313–41.

Morrissey, O. 1993. "The Mixing of Aid and Trade Policies." *World Economy* 16 (1): 69–84.

Neumayer, E. 2003. "The Determinants of Aid Allocation by Regional Multilateral Development Banks and United Nations Agencies." *International Studies Quarterly* 47 (1): 101–22.

Nielson, D., and M. Tierney. 2003. "Delegation to International Organizations: Agency Theory and World Bank Environmental Reform." *International Organization* 57 (2): 241–76.

Nunn, N., and N. Qian. 2014. "US Food Aid and Civil Conflict." *American Economic Review* 104 (6): 1630–66.

Osei, R., O. Morrissey, and T. Lloyd. 2004. "The Nature of Aid and Trade Relationships." *European Journal of Development Research* 16 (2): 354–74.

Regan, P. M. 2000. *Civil War and Foreign Powers*. Ann Arbor: University of Michigan Press.

———. 2002. "Third-Party Interventions and the Duration of Intrastate Conflicts." *Journal of Conflict Resolution* 46 (1): 55–73.

Rodrik, D. 1996. "Why Is There Multilateral Lending?" In *Annual World Bank Conference on Development Economics, 1995*, edited by M. Bruno and B. Pleskovic, 167–93. Washington, DC: World Bank.

———. 2019. "Putting Global Governance in Its Place." NBER Working Paper 26213, National Bureau of Economic Research, Cambridge, MA.

Ruggeri, A., H. Dorussen, and T. Gizelis. 2017. "Winning the Peace Locally: UN Peacekeeping and Local Conflict." *International Organization* 71 (1): 163–85.

Saideman, S. M. 2001. *The Ties That Divide: Ethnic Politics, Foreign Policy and International Conflict*. New York: Columbia University Press.

Salehyan, I. 2010. "The Delegation of War to Rebel Organizations." *Journal of Conflict Resolution* 54 (3): 493–515.

Salehyan, I., and K. S. Gleditsch. 2006. "Refugees and the Spread of Civil War." *International Organization* 60 (2): 335–66.

Sambanis, N., and M. Doyle. 2007. "No Easy Choices: Estimating the Effects of the United Nations Peacekeeping." *International Studies Quarterly* 51 (1): 217–26.

Sawyer, K., K. G. Cunningham, and W. Reed. 2017. "The Role of External Support in Civil War Termination." *Journal of Conflict Resolution* 61 (6): 1174–1202.

Schultz, Kenneth A. 2010. "War as an Enforcement Problem: Interstate Conflict over Rebel Support in Civil Wars." *International Organization* 64 (2): 281–312.

Svensson, J. 2000. "Foreign Aid and Rent-Seeking." *Journal of International Economics* 51 (2): 437–61.

Tan-Mullins, M., G. Mohan, and M. Power. 2010. "Redefining 'Aid' in the China-Africa Context." *Development and Change* 41 (5): 857–81.

Torsvik, G. 2005. "Foreign Economic Aid: Should Donors Cooperate?" *Journal of Development Economics* 77 (2): 503–15.

United Nations and World Bank. 2018. *Pathways for Peace: Inclusive Approaches to Preventing Violent Conflict*. Washington, DC: World Bank.

Voeten, E., A. Strezhnev, and M. Bailey. 2009. "United Nations General Assembly Voting Data." https://dataverse.harvard.edu/dataset.xhtml?persistentId =doi:10.7910/DVN/LEJUQZ.

Wagner, D. 2003. "Aid and Trade: An Empirical Study." *Journal of the Japanese and International Economies* 17 (2): 153–73.

Walter, B. 2002. *Committing to Peace: The Successful Settlement of Civil Wars*. Princeton, NJ: Princeton University Press.

Weitzman, M. L. 1980. "The 'Ratchet Principle' and Performance Incentives." *Bell Journal of Economics* 11 (1): 302–08.

White, P. B., D. E. Cunningham, and K. Beardsley. 2018. "Where, When, and How Does the UN Work to Prevent Civil War in Self-Determination Disputes?" *Journal of Peace Research* 55 (3): 380–94.

Wood, R. M., J. D. Kathman, and S. E. Gent. 2012. "Armed Intervention and Civilian Victimization in Intrastate Conflicts." *Journal of Peace Research* 49 (5): 647–60.

Younas, J. 2008. "Motivation for Bilateral Aid Allocation: Altruism or Trade Benefits?" *European Journal of Political Economy* 24 (3): 661–74.